A CUP OF COMFORT

for Dog Lovers II

More stories that celebrate
the boundless energy,
love, and devotion of our
canine companions

Edited by Colleen Sell

Aadamsmedia
Avon, Massachusetts

For my first-born grandson, Scott,
and his first dog, Nash

Copyright © 2009 by F+W Media, Inc.
All rights reserved. This book, or parts thereof, may not be
reproduced in any form without permission from the publisher;
exceptions are made for brief excerpts used in published reviews.

A *Cup of Comfort*® is a registered trademark of F+W Media, Inc.

Published by
Adams Media, a division of F+W Media, Inc.
57 Littlefield Street, Avon, MA 02322 U.S.A.
www.adamsmedia.com and *www.cupofcomfort.com*

ISBN 10: 1-60550-089-5
ISBN 13: 978-1-60550-089-8
Printed in the United States of America.

J I H G F E D C B A

Library of Congress Cataloging-in-Publication Data
is available from the publisher.

This publication is designed to provide accurate and authoritative information with regard to the subject matter covered. It is sold with the
understanding that the publisher is not engaged in rendering legal,
accounting, or other professional advice. If legal advice or other expert
assistance is required, the services of a competent professional person
should be sought.

—From a *Declaration of Principles* jointly adopted by
a Committee of the American Bar Association and
a Committee of Publishers and Associations

Many of the designations used by manufacturers and sellers to distin-
guish their products are claimed as trademarks. Where those designations appear in this book and Adams Media was aware of a trademark
claim, the designations have been printed with initial capital letters.

This book is available at quantity discounts for bulk purchases.
For information, please call 1-800-289-0963.

Contents

Acknowledgments

My sincere thanks to the fabulous folks at Adams Media, who always come through with the direction and support it takes to produce and publish books of quality.

I am especially beholding to my right-hand gal, *Cup of Comfort*® project editor Meredith O'Hayre; my long-time colleague and *Cup of Comfort's*® creator, Paula Munier (a dog lover if ever there was one); Jacquinn Williams, the *Cup of Comfort*® publicist; Ashley Vierra, the book's designer; and publisher Karen Cooper.

Thanks to the authors whose stories grace these pages, not only for their great words but also for being such great people to work with.

Thanks, too, to the authors whose submissions did not make it into the book. Your terrific stories made my job difficult but all the more enjoyable.

Thank you, dear reader, for joining us in this celebration of man's best friend.

And thanks to Woodstock, who has made a dog lover out of me.

Introduction

"The one absolutely unselfish friend that man can have in this selfish world, the one that never deserts him, the one that never proves ungrateful or treacherous, is his dog . . . He will kiss the hand that has no food to offer; he will lick the wounds and sores that come in encounter with the roughness of the world . . . When all other friends desert, he remains."

—*George G. Vest*

My dog, Woodstock, loves me. With all his heart. Unconditionally. I know that, just as surely as I know my name, because he shows me every chance he gets. No matter how little attention I pay to him or how grumpy I am, the Woodster always greets me with a spring in his step, an "I'm interested" cock of his head, a glint of pure happiness in his eyes, and the sweetest smile.

Woody would defend me with his life. He would chase off a bear, face down a cougar, take on a pack of coyotes, or take out a raccoon to protect me. I know, because he has.

If he sensed that I was sick or hurt or that my heart was broken, that little border collie–Australian shepherd mix would jump an eight-foot fence to help me or run to my husband barking and pulling at him to come quick or sit outside my window howling in commiseration. I know, because he has.

He's never too tired or too busy to go for a walk or to play catch with me. And never complains or sulks when I'm too tired or too busy to go for a walk or to play catch with him.

He's got my back and he's there for me, 110 percent, no strings attached, no matter what.

As friends go, you can't get any better than that.

I like to think that Woodstock is an exceptional dog. That his bravery, devotion, friendliness, intuitiveness, and intelligence are unique to my wicked-smart sweetheart of a dog. That his connection to me and to my family is extraordinary. In fact, I was convinced of that . . . until I read the tsunami of stories we received for this book and its predecessor, *A*

Cup of Comfort® *for Dog Lovers* (2007). Now I know better. Now I know that the bond between humans and dogs runs long and deep, extending far back in time and to millions of people and dogs the world over. That the friendship between people and dogs is so prevalent does not make it any less special. Indeed, it is something to celebrate.

So we decided that one anthology of stories celebrating the special relationship between dogs and humans wasn't enough, and A *Cup of Comfort*® *for Dog Lovers II* was born. I hope you'll enjoy it.

—*Colleen Sell*

Penny's Protection

I heard the kitchen door slam and then Dad's clunky footfalls. I lay there in the dark trying to sleep. At seven years old, I was afraid, mostly of the dark, but I also imagined mean, awful men breaking in and hurting me. If only my dog Penny could sleep with me. Penny, my black Lab, was outside in a cold, concrete pen all by herself. If she'd been in bed with me, I'd have snuggled with her and stroked her head. If Penny were there in my room, she'd protect me, but I was alone.

My brothers, Jeff and Barry, and I had just gone to bed. Mother was in the kitchen folding laundry.

Dad yelled, "What the hell are you doing?"

"Laundry," mother explained in a low voice.

My bedroom was the closest to the living room and the kitchen. I heard everything. I heard fear mixed with anger.

Dad slurred his words. "That's a stupid thing to be doing at this time of night." He fumbled over "time of night."

"You've been drinking, haven't you?" Mother said more forcefully.

"I don't have to explain myself to you. How about fixing me something to eat?"

Dad's fist slammed down. I imagined the terror on Mom's face and how cautious her next move might be. Or was I planning my own next move?

I lay in bed, petrified like a mummy, unable to move, unable to scream. Why wasn't Penny allowed in the house? I slid down under the covers and rubbed my lips back and forth over the ribbon trim of the blanket. It was comforting. Then I found the place where the ribbon trim had torn away from the blanket. I rubbed the ribbon between my fingers over and over and slid the silkiness and smoothness across my lips. I pretended that the silkiness was Penny's ears and that I was safely snuggled next to her.

Mother tried to stand up to Dad, even though he was drunk. "I'm not fixing any more dinner tonight. If you want something you'll have to fix it yourself."

Dad's voice thundered. "When I ask for something, damn it, you'd better get it. Do you understand? I've had it with you."

He stumbled into the hallway outside my bed-room door. I huddled down deeper into my covers.

Dad kept yelling. "You'd better listen to me and get damn used to it too. I'm the boss around here and what I say goes."

I could hear his body thud against the wall. There was shuffling and banging, and then *pow!* The wall next to me shook. The noise was deafen-ing. I could hear Mom scoot the metal kitchen chair away from the table. Her footsteps got louder, as if she were walking toward the hallway.

"Now, look at what you've done," she was saying. "There's a hole right through the wall. I'm telling you, the drinking has to stop."

There was more scuffling and a bump against the wall. I imagined Mom lying on the floor, bleed-ing. Now I was really afraid. What if he killed her? Then he could do whatever he pleased to me. At least with Mother around he had somebody else to pick on.

I couldn't count on Mother for much protection. She was too afraid of Dad herself. I wanted her to protect me. I really did. But she never kept Dad from bullying, especially when he was drunk. I was too young to understand all that was wrong in our house, but I knew one thing: Penny loved me. Penny would protect me. I lay in bed barely breathing, wishing my dog lay next to me. I cried softly, knowing she was shivering in her pen, alone.

Mother had given up her religion, her family, and her future to marry Dad. My grandparents came from Italy, where Grandpa worked in the Washington coal mines until he died from black lung. Grandma died when Mother was four, and her older sister had raised her. The Catholic Church had been the center of Mom's life. At one time, Mother had even wanted to be a nun. She told me that. I could hardly believe she'd given up so much to marry Dad.

Under the covers, I curled into a ball and waited. My baby brother must have stayed asleep, because I didn't hear crying. Were my two older brothers asleep or awake? Jeff was just a year ahead of me, Barry three years older. They must both have been awake too.

The arguing and yelling continued, swelling into a rage that filled the whole house. I tried not to listen, but I couldn't stop myself from hearing. I held my hands over my ears, trying to muffle the shouts. Just like every other time, I felt helpless. Like all the other times, there was no escape.

I couldn't stop thinking of Penny. "Penny, Penny, I need you," I whispered. I was glad she wasn't in the house. She hated yelling. But I also felt desperate for Penny's warm fur and comfort.

Dad's heavy, unstable steps clomped toward the back door. "I should just kill you, poison you. That's what I should do." Mother didn't answer Dad's threat.

Then I heard sobbing. Mom's cries went on and on, interspersed with wails and gasps, like someone trying desperately to catch their breath. I was sure Mom had slumped to the floor or the couch. I could hear Dad pacing as the sobs continued. As long as Mom was crying, she was still alive.

But she couldn't help me. A chilling thought entered my mind. *What would I do if he came into my room?* There was no escape route. *Would he hit me? Would he kill me?* My thoughts tumbled over and over. Fear touched every bone, every muscle, and every cell in my body. I lay there very, very still, almost not breathing. All I could think of was that if Penny were there, she would attack him. If necessary, she'd sic Dad good.

The sobbing continued. I pictured Mom red-eyed and lost, lying on the couch in her crumpled house dress. I pictured Penny trying to break out of her pen to get to me.

My brothers' bedroom door opened. Dad bellowed, "Wake up, wake up. Get up now and get out in the living room."

I knew I was next. My door opened. "Wake up and get out here right now."

Dad half-pushed, half-shoved the three of us into the living room. He stood before us, swaying unsteadily. "If you've ever prayed, you better pray now," he said. "Get on your knees. You'd better pray that your mom makes it through this."

I glanced over at Mom on the couch, unable to stop sobbing or even notice us. Dad said something about her having a nervous breakdown.

My brothers, in their flannel pajamas printed with cowboys on horses, got on their knees. I followed in my red flannel nightgown. We knelt around the big, bulky, maroon overstuffed chair. The upholstery's paisley pattern was raised. Over and over, I followed the pattern with my finger.

Tears ran down Jeff's cheeks. Barry and I both fought back tears. My insides churned, and I told myself, *Don't cry, don't cry.* I knelt on one side of the chair, Jeff on the other, and Barry in the middle. Each padded arm had a wooden center on its front with a fluid design carved in it. I ran my hand down the side, feeling the wooden design and thinking how different the upholstery felt.

Dad interrupted my thoughts. "Your mother could die tonight. Pray and pray hard."

We all bowed our heads. The room was absolutely silent except for mother's moans. *Would he really kill Mom?* With Dad, you never knew. Dad forced us all to belong to the Southern Baptist church. Sometimes my dad was saved and sometimes he wasn't. Tonight he wasn't.

We knelt for what seemed like hours, each of us afraid to move, afraid to get up and go to bed. Finally, Barry's head slumped down on the chair's big, squishy cushion. He'd fallen asleep, right there on his knees. I leaned my head against the chair's arm; it smelled like Mom's face cream. As the minutes wore on, the sobbing quieted. Dad sat on the floor next to Mother. He told us to go to bed. I nudged Barry, and all three of us shuffled down the hall and into our rooms.

I lay awake for what seemed like forever, listening, waiting. Finally, I heard Dad coax Mother, and they both went to bed.

The house fell silent. The silence felt heavy, like a weight pressing down on me. When I was sure everybody was asleep, I got up and tiptoed to the back door. I turned the knob very slowly, making sure it made no sound.

When I got outside, I looked up at the explosion of stars in the sky. The slight breeze raised my nightgown like an umbrella around me, and the grass was cool and slightly wet between my toes. There was a sliver of moon on the horizon. I stood still for a few moments, looking up, and then I hurried to Penny's kennel and let her out. I didn't dare take her into my bedroom, so I tiptoed in the back door and led her down the stairs into the basement.

The basement staircase was pitch-black. I felt around for the switch, and one bare bulb lit up at the bottom of the stairs. Penny and I made our way down. The furnace wasn't on, but its huge belly cast spooky shadows everywhere. I made my way behind the furnace, where the washer and dryer stood. I found a pile of old blankets in the corner and sat down. Penny laid her head in my lap, and I caressed her behind the ears.

Finally, my eyes closed and I felt my body relax. Penny snuggled close to me, and for a minute, I felt small and yet so peaceful.

Dad's drunken rages worsened as the years went by. Penny spent her life by my side. She waited at the corner for me every day after school. She knew exactly when I would arrive. We raced down the hill together and shared our afternoons in each other's company. She was my confidant, my best friend. When the words ripped my self-esteem to shreds, she was there embracing me with her presence. She built me up with her love. Because of Penny, I survived.

Eventually, I grew old enough to stand up for myself and I left.

In the basement corner, Penny was my comfort. She loved me more than anybody else. I stroked her glossy black coat over and over. I kissed her between her big brown eyes. I told her how much I loved her and how scary the evening had been. She licked my hand and my face. Her eyes full of compassion and kindness, she promised she'd never hurt me. I was absolutely sure of that. The night we prayed for Mother's life, Penny saved mine.

—Linda Stork

Blue Ribbon Winner

Life among a family of storytellers guaranteed that our collie would not become the neighborhood dog who had lost his leg to cancer. Sure, we had started with the truth, but the medical jargon and depressing details exhausted us. Not to mention, we are narrators who take pleasure in weaving extraordinary stories, so Dexter's tale of survival would be no different.

Catching a glimpse of Dexter, others would say, "Oh, how sad," or "Poor dog," and these responses grew tiresome, even a bit annoying. As a stray dog and a scrapper who'd survived on the streets before we adopted him, Dexter was far from sad or poor. We knew that he deserved to be held in wonder, not smothered in pity, when people discovered the reason behind the missing leg.

"Why does your dog only have three legs?" the boy asked, pointing over the fence.

Our family looked at one another to see who would tackle the routine question. My daughter, Piper, stepped forward. Sitting on the patio, I leafed through a magazine while waiting to hear Piper's account of the cancerous tumor that had led to the removal of our beloved pet's leg. To my surprise, Piper swiftly substituted the words bear trap for tumor—and so began our family's quest for the most creative narrative.

My mouth gaped open then snapped shut like the steel jaws that had apparently left Dexter in peril. Drawing upon details from our recent trip to the Smoky Mountains, Piper wove her tale of deception, using the mountainous landscape as the setting. The boy clung to my daughter's words as she described Dexter's numerous attempts to free himself from the deadly trap. Piper challenged the limits of credibility by claiming that Dexter kept warm in the cold, dark woods overnight by digging a hole and covering himself with fallen leaves, until he could be rescued the next morning.

"But how did he dig a hole with the trap on his leg?" the boy asked.

With as much curiosity as the boy, I waited for Piper's response.

"He had three other legs, remember?"

Her simple answer made sense in a way, considering the miraculous feats Dexter had accomplished since his surgery. Like how he now managed to run up and down the stairwell, following his initial game of doggie pinball in which we all held our breath while he slammed from side to side. Or how Dexter had learned to avoid lifting his hind leg on the same side of his missing front leg, lest he topple sideways like a cow in a pasture filled with bored teenagers. We thought it best for Dexter to figure things out, forgoing modifications to our household such as a lift, special bed, wagon, or ramp. Dexter's tools of survival consisted of his raw determination and inner-strength. I suppose these heartwarming details could have been added to our stories, but we preferred epic tales filled with adventure and excitement.

The boy seemed satisfied with Piper's answer and left. Once home, he would surely retell the story to his family, perhaps adding a thunderstorm or pack of wolves to heighten the suspense. Where the deceit would end was anyone's guess.

Now, don't get me wrong, our family never encouraged blatant lying just for the sake of lying. We considered such untruths to be a form of entertainment for the inquisitive. Over time, the stories became a family contest, and a blue ribbon awaited the person who concocted the most entertaining tale.

The following week, my son, Holden, tried his hand at storytelling. To Holden's disadvantage, his audience was an adult; more astute than a child, thus harder to convince. I listened as Holden provided the details for the curious passerby.

"The gun went *bang, bang, bang!* While the robber shot Dexter in the leg, Frodo hid in the corner."

Credibility points for adding our other dog into the story, I thought as Holden continued.

"And then Dexter lunged at the man with the gun, knocking it out of his hands. Dexter growled and snarled at the robber, protecting us until the police came to arrest the bad guy."

"Really?" the woman challenged as her belief in the story appeared to wane.

"Yep. The robber's still in prison, you know." Pride splashed across Holden's face, and he looked at his sister, who nodded assent.

"Hmm, interesting," the woman said as she left.

Now, my husband Michael held a closer relationship with the truth than the rest of us, convincing me that he couldn't stray far from reality. He looked at our neighbor and smiled.

"Well, an old college buddy of mine likes to sail the Eastern Coastline each summer. I joined him and took old Dex along, thinking he'd enjoy the fresh air." Michael pointed to Dexter. "So, I'm heading below deck for a minute, and the next thing I know, a shark jumps up and snatches the leg clean off. And just like that, it was gone."

Unbelievable, I thought. Not the outlandish story, per se, but rather my husband's reckless abandonment of the truth. Clearly, he would have said anything to garner the blue ribbon.

"You're kidding me, aren't you?" the neighbor said, chuckling.

"Have you ever known me to lie?" Michael asked.

Our family shook our heads in unison.

"And, you'll never believe this," my husband started again, and I immediately flashed him the don't-go-over-the-top stare. Michael settled for the story he had presented and merely added, "Dexter can still play ball."

Over the next several weeks, the pressure mounted as I tried to imagine a story that would beat the previous tales spun by my children and husband, but my accounts of the missing leg seemed silly or contrived. Frustrated, I nearly gave up.

"Hey, what happened to your dog?" the teenage girl said while standing with her younger sister.

"What?" I asked, secretly hoping they'd lose interest and move on.

"You know, the leg . . ." she said.

My family turned to me and waited for an answer. I sighed and resigned myself to the truth of the cancerous tumor for lack of a more creative response. "Well," I started.

My son patted my arm in encouragement, prompting me to switch course.

"Our dog has always loved the children's birthday parties," I continued. "So, when the magician at Piper's party asked for a volunteer from the audience, we offered up Dexter." I smiled wickedly as I pictured my husband pinning the blue ribbon on my blouse. "The magician placed our dog in the metal box and then pulled out his long saw."

I looked at my family, noticing the twinkle of deception in their eyes in recognition of my efforts. "You can imagine our surprise when the magician opened the box and the leg was gone." I briefly lowered my head for dramatic effect. "How were we to know that he was an apprentice magician? The man didn't know whether to be terrified or proud of his performance."

The girls looked at one another in dismay, then turned their attention back to me.

"But, needless to say, we got a refund."

The two girls scurried off without a rebuttal, so my family gave me a bonus point for credibility.

In hindsight, perhaps our storytelling eased our pain after Dexter's cancer diagnosis and helped to offset the ongoing fear of having to euthanize him if the cancer returned. The first few weeks after the surgery, we helplessly watched Dexter hop from place to place. His inability to fetch a ball and his need to eat while lying down left us wondering if we had made the right decision. But when such actions became commonplace, we no longer grieved. Instead, we rejoiced in his resiliency and wove our peculiar yarns to match his bravery. Our family believed that Dexter enjoyed the stories of his heroic deeds and narrow escapes from death during his spectacular adventures.

As for Dexter, well, he had his own story to tell—one of simple truths. Given his ability to overcome adversity, to courageously explore unknown territory, and to remain flexible in the throes of life's challenges, it became clear to us that it was our stalwart dog who deserved the blue ribbon.

—Cathi LaMarche

The Recruiting of Sergeant Berg

My father leaned against the kitchen counter, waiting for my mother to finish the phone call from Maggie, a widow who lived a mile west of us. His hand went from his winter-coat pocket to the doorknob and back, because he was impatient to start the farm chores. He would have left once he had eaten breakfast if Mama hadn't motioned for him to stay and added a frown as an explanation point.

"What'd she want?" he asked when Mama hung up the receiver.

"To know if we'd gotten a dog to replace Lady. There's a stray in her garage, and she's afraid to get it out by herself. She thinks it'd make us a good watch dog."

"Or to get rid of." He looked at me. "We'll need dog food. And Lady's old leash."

I pulled on my overshoes and hurried out into the frigid February morning. The year before, my brother, Craig, had joined the Army to avoid the draft and beat the odds of ending up in Vietnam like the other farm boys in our community. When Uncle Sam's letter arrived, Daddy and a recruiter advised Craig to enlist for an extra year's service and to receive training in aircraft mechanics instead of infantry. This resulted in his being stationed in Panama and in my promotion from fifteen-year-old kid sister to my father's weekend and summer farm hand.

After Daddy and I scattered hay in the pastures for our cattle, we stopped at Maggie's early 1900s Oklahoma farmhouse. Her car was parked in the open-ended shed she used for a garage.

As Daddy peered into the unlit building, I asked, "See him?"

"No, probably scared."

Most strays were timid. The sad fact city folks didn't understand when they dumped a dog in the country was that their pet would either starve, be killed by coyotes, or get shot for chasing livestock. Few found a home.

"Morning," Maggie called from her back door. "You want him?"

"Haven't seen him yet," Daddy said.

"He's there. Growled when I went to back my car out. Scared the living daylights out of me. He's got a collar, but I couldn't see a tag."

"What kind is he?"

"Don't know. Too dark in there to tell."

"Joanie," Daddy said. "Get the dog food and the leash. We'll see if we can coax him out."

We inched our way toward the back of the shed until a dark shadow stood and rumbled like a semi headed down the highway. I jumped behind Daddy.

"Easy, boy," Daddy said quietly as if he were talking to a nervous mother cow. "Bet you're hungry. Come here."

With Daddy's enticing, the shadow emerged as the biggest German shepherd I had ever seen. It stretched halfway across the garage to sniff the bowl of food Daddy set on the floor, but when Daddy clicked the leash on the collar ring, the menacing dog wagged its tail and looked up at us with an open mouth I would have sworn was a grin.

"Hey, you're a good boy," Daddy said as he ruffled his fur.

We searched the newspaper every day for a lost pet ad, because Mama insisted a German shepherd that big and good-looking belonged to someone, her way of saying he scared her. But after a week's worth of loveable tail-wagging, he won her over and she suggested, if we planned to keep him, then we'd better name him. It took Daddy less than two seconds to come up with "Sarge," which made me think he had it picked out the morning we coaxed the dog from Maggie's garage.

"If there ever was a dog that looked like a sergeant, it's him," Daddy said with a single nod.

I should have known. Daddy had been a sergeant in the Air Corps during World War II and sometimes had these cloudy-eyed moments when he wished he had stayed in the military instead of returning home to farm. He had come down with that same look the day my brother left for the Army.

We soon learned Sarge was an obedient stray, trotting beside us as we walked, sitting at our feet when we stopped, and lying down on command. Every morning when Daddy went to feed, Sarge rode in the back of our old '57 Ford pickup and not once did he bark, snarl, or make a run at the cattle, which would have been unforgivable on our farm. I loved his perpetual "grin" and his nuzzling me until I scratched him behind his ears. Mama called him the biggest baby of a dog that she'd ever owned.

During June, we left Sarge at home while my mother and I helped my father harvest the wheat crop. Every morning, I'd fill the pickup's gas tank before I headed to the field by the unpaved back roads to avoid getting caught for underage driving. With the sun still nested on the eastern horizon one morning, I hand-pumped fuel from a fifty-five gallon drum Daddy kept behind the barn. Half asleep, I had left the truck door open to listen to the radio and didn't notice Sarge until he had jumped into the cab. I scowled at the dewy brown paw prints he'd stamped on the new seat cover Mama had put over the frayed original, and I sensed a lecture coming when she saw the damage.

"Out," I said. Sarge grinned and ignored the command from someone he probably considered a mere private in rank. After I topped off the tank, I tried to convince him again.

"Out of there. Now!"

I reached into the truck to give his collar a good yank, straining my elbow but not budging him from the bench seat. Since Daddy and Mama had gone ahead and would worry if I didn't follow soon, I grabbed the fur of either side of Sarge's neck, braced my foot on the running board of the pickup, and heaved.

"Come on," I groaned as I pulled him across the seat. "I have to get to the field."

Without warning, Sarge surrendered in our game of tug-of-war, and I fell flat on my back, dazed and looking up at his open mouth.

"Get off of me!" I yelled. "Beat it! You've got dog breath." I scrambled into the pickup, only to have him rest his paws on the door and stick his nose through the window. I shoved his head away and rolled up the glass. Our last watchdog, Lady, had lived up to her dignified name. It appeared Sarge's getting in my face was his way of living up to his.

In Oklahoma, drought usually begins at the end of harvest. With it too dry to work the fields, Daddy caught up on chores around the farm while Mama and I canned beans and tomatoes from our garden. We lived at a slower pace and ate Mama's "gourmet" meals instead of sandwiches gulped on the run. After Daddy said grace over supper one evening, Mama started passing the mashed potatoes and fried chicken around the table.

"I had to read the meter for the electric company," she said. "I heard honking and went to see what was the matter. It was a new man, and he claimed Sarge wouldn't let him out of the truck. You'd think OG&E'd hire somebody that wasn't afraid of dogs."

"Arthur said the same thing happened to him a couple of weeks ago," Daddy said as he glanced at me.

The pickle I was eating hit the back of my throat. "But that's what Sarge is supposed to do," I said between coughs. "Scare people."

"Not neighbors." Daddy set his fork and knife beside his plate. "I saw an ad in the paper the other day. The military is looking for dogs to train. They're offering up to a hundred and fifty dollars."

"A hundred and fifty dollars for a dog?" I asked.

"That's what the ad said."

He would know. Everyday, he read the newspaper from front to back, including fillers, obituaries, and want ads. Still, I couldn't believe it, not even for a German shepherd as good as Sarge.

"We can't have a dog that might bite somebody," he said.

"He isn't mean. He just acts that way. He wouldn't bite a flea." After all, I practically had skinned him alive trying to get him out of the pickup.

"If they took him, he'd be in the Air Force," Daddy said as a cloudy-eyed look came over him. "What better life for a dog?"

Once Daddy mentioned "Air Force," I knew I had a better chance of changing the wishbone on my plate into a wing than changing his mind.

On Saturday, we dressed in the same town clothes we wore the day we'd left my brother on the steps of the federal building. This time, I hoped Mama wouldn't cry. Daddy had Sarge tied in the pickup bed for the long ride to Tinker Air Force Base in Midwest City, an hour and a half from home.

When we arrived, we followed other owners leading their collies, poodles, and mutts to a table set up in an empty field. Daddy signed the waiting list. One by one, a sergeant summoned owners, gave their dogs a fleeting look, then promptly sent them home. A Doberman managed to make it as far as the physical exam before he failed. All the while, the sergeant and an airman kept eyeing us and studying the list.

"Berg?" the airman asked, as if not quite sure how to pronounce our name, but he smiled when Daddy approached the table with Sarge. "Sir, may I?"

The airman took the leash from Daddy and led Sarge to the veterinarian. Once Sarge had passed the physical, the airman gave the collar a tug and they marched in lockstep toward a large oak. Ten feet away, Sarge's ears perked. The airman unsnapped the leash. When a fat man in a padded suit ran from behind the tree, the fur on our German shepherd's back rose higher than a razor-backed hog's. Then Sarge lunged, and Mama and I, along with the rest of the crowd, pulled back in awe as he worried his prey around like a cotton-tailed rabbit. The fat man finally yelled to call off the dog.

"I want him, sir," he said, struggling to his feet.

A lieutenant with a clipboard walked over to Daddy. "We'll be proud to have your dog. Full price of a hundred and fifty dollars. If you'd sign these papers, I'll get you the money."

"Sir?" the airman asked when Daddy's hand shook taking the offered pen. "Didn't you know you had a trained attack dog?"

Daddy stuttered, "I figured he had been trained, but . . ." His voice fell away.

That's when I remembered how I'd grabbed that lovable dog's fur to pull him across the seat of our old '57 Ford pickup. That lovable trained attack dog. The hair on my neck twittered.

As Sarge trotted past us to join the Air Force, he gave us one last knowing grin. Mama stood there wiping her eyes while Daddy watched Sarge with that cloudy look in his. I returned Sarge's grin and waved goodbye.

—Joan King

Eric's Champion

At age seven, my son got the foolish notion that what he really wanted for his fast approaching eighth birthday was a dog. Even more foolish, I got him one. At the time, I thought it would help. He was homesick and unhappy about our cross-country move to California and was becoming a stubborn and combative discipline problem.

I wanted to go about this pet selection in a sensible manner, so I asked Dr. Mitchell, our cats' veterinarian, to suggest a good breed of dog for an almost eight-year-old boy. He recommended a trip to the pound, where the child could choose the one he liked.

"Children generally select a pet that mirrors their own personality," he said.

I should have paid more attention to that remark.

We went to the pound, where Eric chose a black and white puppy, quite small but still too big for its funny little legs. We paid the pound their suggested donation and headed for the veterinarian's office to make sure that this was a healthy animal. Champion, Champ for short, received his name en route to the vet's and was ready for his physical—we thought.

Champ did not agree and, after meeting the veterinarian, bit him. Just as Dr. Mitchell had predicted, Eric chose a pet to match his personality and now I had two behavioral problems.

While the nurse applied the band-aid to his bleeding finger, Dr. Mitchell pronounced Champ a healthy animal but an unfortunate mixing of breeds. He was part terrier—note, the small sturdy body and typical black and white coat. This is a breed known to be feisty, originally bred to ferret out small prey, bite deep, and hold on tight until their masters could dispose of the catch. In other words, terriers tend to be chasers and biters. The other part of Champ was dachshund—note, the short stubby legs and splayed "Charlie Chaplin" front paws. The prevailing trait of dachshunds is that they're stubborn. So we had a feisty, stubborn dog who would fight a lot and be difficult to make behave. Champ and Eric were soul mates for sure.

I didn't need another discipline problem around the house. I needed an obedience school for boy and dog. I reasoned that enrolling Champ in the local park's dog-obedience class, with Eric responsible for putting his dog through the required steps of the training, would benefit them both.

And so we arrived at the park early one evening, an enthusiastic mother dragging a reluctant boy and dog to the registration desk. I admit Champ looked out of place and a little ridiculous amongst the pure-bred Afghans, German shepherds, and Great Danes in line ahead of us. Eric's eyes wandered longingly over to the adjoining ball field, where a baseball game was in progress. Champ tugged at his leash, eager to sniff up the other enrollees.

At last it was our turn.

"Animal's name?" the voice behind the desk barked at me.

"Champion," I managed to mumble without looking down at the ridiculous specimen beside me.

"Breed?" the voice barked again.

"Mutt," I gulped.

"He is not a mutt. The term for mixed-breeds is 'all American,'" the voice said.

I looked down at Champion, the all-American dog, now yanking at his leash, snarling and barking at his more refined classmates, who ignored him, and

I tried, I really tried, to feel pride in this new designation. It was hopeless.

"Owner?" the voice asked.

"Eric Colby," I said and nodded toward my son standing beside me with his head craned in the direction of the ball field. I couldn't wait to hand him the leash and retreat into the background.

The woman behind the desk rose slightly from her seat to peer down at the skinny little boy by my side, then plunked back into her chair.

"He's too young. Trainers must be at least twelve years old."

Eric brightened immediately. "It's okay, Mom. I'll watch the ball game while you train Champ." And off he ran.

Champ quickly proved he was no champion. The instructor, a burly female ex-Marine drill sergeant, or good imitation thereof, ordered us to line up with our canines. I was relieved to see a tan boxer wander out of line as far as her leash would allow. Champ wasn't going to be the only problem dog in the class, after all.

"Get that bitch back into line!" the instructor bellowed.

Several of us were shocked at her language. She read it in our faces.

With a sneer, she said, "Male canines are 'dogs.' Females are called 'bitches.'"

We felt duly chastised for our ignorance. We were stupid, and Caroline, as she told us to call her, was our superior, to be obeyed without question. Fine with me. Oh please, please let it be fine with Champ.

It wasn't. He wouldn't sit. He wouldn't stay. He wouldn't heel. But he didn't get yelled at. Caroline yelled at me, as if I were the one misbehaving. I don't know why. I was dutifully pulling the leash up while pressing down on Champ's rump and saying, "Sit." Once he sat, I was dutifully putting my hand on his nose and saying, "Stay," as I walked away from him. I was dutifully drawing the leash tightly to me while walking with him and saying, "Heel." I was doing everything she ordered us to do. Champ was the one ignoring commands and doing as he pleased, but Caroline ignored him.

Sarge (as I secretly called her) ignored him until question time at the end of the session. We sat in chairs lined up against the chain-link fence at the edge of the yard, our canines at our feet for the larger dogs, on our laps for the smaller ones. Caroline stood before us and asked if anyone had a particular problem with their animal that they would like addressed.

The man with the German shepherd said his dog had a habit of barking that annoyed his neighbors. Caroline approached the dog.

"You can cure a dog of barking," she assured us. "When your dog barks," she said as she raised her arm into the air, "you bring up your hand and say 'Out!' while you deliver a sharp karate chop to his nose." She brought her arm down sharply as she spoke, striking the unsuspecting shepherd on his snout and crumpling him into a whimpering ball.

"Now, with a dog this size," she continued as she approached the tiny teacup poodle on its owner's lap in the next chair, "you cannot do that. You would break the animal's nose. However," she said as her hand went up again, though not as high, "you can accomplish the same result with a stern rap using just two fingers." She demonstrated on the poodle's pointy snout, producing a high-pitched agonizing yelp from the creature.

Champ was on my lap in the next chair, and Caroline was on a roll. "Now, even with a dog this size," she began, once again raising her two fingers, this time above Champ's head. She didn't get to finish. Champ lunged at her upraised hand and bit it.

This time the yelp came from Caroline. She lowered her arm and examined her lightly bloodied fingers, then pointed accusingly at the feisty terrier/ stubborn dachshund/all-American canine sharing my chair, and addressed the class.

"This is an incorrigible animal," she announced. "Just as there are incorrigible children, there are incorrigible animals."

I wondered if the comparison to certain children was aimed at my son. Was she saying, like owner, like pet? She wouldn't have been far from the truth in those days, except that Eric hadn't bitten anyone, at least, not that I knew of.

"I will not graduate that dog," Caroline concluded, still pointing at Champ and glaring at me.

We were being expelled! Kicked out of obedience school. I rose, still clutching Champ, my face burning, and rushed away. I collected my protesting son—the baseball game wasn't over yet—and hurried us all into the car.

"How did it go?" my husband Dick asked when we got home.

I told him the whole horrible story of the "how to train a dog not to bark" episode and how ashamed I was at Champ's behavior.

"Ashamed?" he questioned. "Why ashamed? It seems to me Champ showed great intelligence. He saw what happened to the German shepherd when the teacher raised her hand above it. Then he saw what happened to the poodle when the teacher raised her hand again. So when she raised her hand above Champ, he was not about to sit there and let the same thing happen to him. That would have been stupid. Then you'd have had a right to be ashamed."

Maybe. But knowing I had an intelligent, incorrigible dog didn't make me feel any better. Champ never did learn to sit or stay when told, and neither did Eric. They remained the best of pals, cut from the same cloth. The only difference was that I still got calls from Eric's teacher, but Caroline was done with us. She never called.

Why did we keep a difficult dog like Champ? Champ didn't judge Eric, scold him, or lecture him. Champ was the only one in the world whom Eric felt understood him. The only one an unhappy little boy could tell his troubles to when the whole world seemed lined up against him. The only one to make a difficult first year in Los Angeles bearable for our homesick son. How could we not keep Champ?

Champion may have been an obedience school drop-out and incorrigible, but he was smart enough to know that, with his help, his buddy Eric would turn out just fine.

—Marcia Rudoff

Dog Asana

I t happens every morning: Caleb, our golden retriever, hears me unfurl my yoga mat and comes running. By the time I've shimmied into my yoga pants, the dog—my faithful and enthusiastic companion in most, if not all, activities—has taken up residence on the cushiony surface where, for the next forty-five minutes or so, I'll put my body through its paces. The "or so" depends on how extensive a practice I plan to perform and how much tummy rubbing will be demanded by this furry creature spread out in all of his seventy-pound glory.

It's only when I crouch to get onto the mat that Caleb considers relinquishing his position. I like to think he's warming the mat for me, but his motives are anything but altruistic. Rather, my companion has placed himself at the epicenter of the exercise area to receive lots of high-quality tummy rubs while I work my way through each sequence of my routine.

Before exiting the mat, Caleb rolls onto his back, legs spread indelicately, and undulates back and forth until I run my hand along the furry stretch between his chest and lower rib cage. More often than not, I'll rub the full length of his underside, pausing to knead his upper chest and lower tummy—areas that seem to be the prime pleasure spots of his body.

"Time to move, golden boy," I announce to the spread-eagled creature before me.

Caleb cocks his head upward, as if to inquire, *Who, me?*

I give him a hard stare. "Move, mister," I say.

He looks at me again. My eyebrows arch, signaling that I really do mean business. Caleb wiggles onto his side, then shifts to his feet. He takes his sweet time. After executing a few ritualistic circles, he plants himself within inches of the edge of the mat and me, his yoga woman.

Before settling into "reclining mountain," the common name of the first pose (or "asana" in yogi-lingo) of my routine, I observe a generous scattering of oversized paw prints pressed into the mat's exterior. They create a floral design, a profusion of pansies.

I move from "reclining mountain" (lying flat on my back, arms at sides) into alternating sides of "knee to chest" asanas (grasping one knee at a time with both hands and bringing it to the chest)—punctuated at each release of the knee by a "hand rubbing the dog belly" maneuver. If I hold any of my poses too long, a large, insistent paw tugs at my arm to remind me that there is, after all, a belly to be rubbed. Or a majestic dog head presses close to mine, two dark brown eyes gazing solemnly at me, conveying the message, *I'm waiting. I'm waiting.* Warm doggy breath puffs against my face, and a moist nose-tip nudges (and smudges) my cheek.

Sometimes Caleb's long tongue snakes out to delicately lick my lips or flick up into my nostrils to indicate that he's more than worthy of a tummy massage. If I don't give in and run my hand along his underside, I'll be subjected to increasingly severe stares. If stares don't produce the desired result, I may get doggy huffs (*What does it take to get a tummy rub around here?*) or groans (*You are causing me unconscionable anguish!*) or, when his frustration reaches the boiling point, baritone growls reminiscent of approaching thunder (*I've had it! Move your hand to my belly now!*).

Getting enough tummy rubs is serious business.

As I work through the remainder of my routine, the moment of ultimate canine gratification finally arrives. The "knees to head" asana signals that it's time for "steal the bandana" in doggy yoga-land. My associate has mastered this exercise through daily practice. No sooner is my head against my knees in a tight fetal position than, with fluidity and precision, Caleb grasps an edge of my hair-band, efficiently tugs it off my head, and munches it into a loose wad.

Now the real fun begins. From my scrunched-up position I shout, "Oh, no! Someone's got my bandana!" followed by variations of "Where's my bandana? Who took my bandana? I need my bandana!" It doesn't really matter what I say as long as I feign shock and outrage at this brazen display of doggy thievery. At this point, Caleb sashays back and forth with my bandana, taunting me but not allowing me to actually grab hold of his prize. Or he'll flip the bandana into the air a time or two, only to snarf it up at my first futile snatch and trot away with his honey-blond plume of a tail wagging impudently. The only thing that would bring him more joy would be my exiting the mat and chasing him through our house, shouting, "I want my bandana! Give me my bandana!"

The rest of my practice is uneventful. By now, my partner has retreated to his bed, where he guards his prize as though it were a cache of diamonds. Heaven help the person (namely, my husband) who tries to take away the bandana, now positioned underneath his muzzle or between his front paws as this sneaky thief catches a few winks.

At the conclusion of my practice, I go looking for my stolen property.

"May I have my bandana?" I ask Caleb politely.

A bribe of liver nips ensures the immediate release of his booty.

"Oh, thank you!" I praise him as I retrieve my headgear. "You took such good care of it! Now it's all ready for me to wear!"

Ignoring doggy drool, I roll the munged-up cloth back into a band and slip it onto my head, where it will remain until it's stolen with canine cunning the following morning.

I know that if I were a truly dedicated yogi, I would have no qualms about sequestering the dog elsewhere. Practicing yoga with a dog who has his own repertoire of asanas is time-consuming and hardly conducive to the proper execution of my poses. But would I ever confine Caleb to another room and miss our daily dose of slightly demented dog-and-woman interaction? You've got to be kidding!

"*Namaste*, good dog," I croon as I bend to scratch behind Caleb's ears.

He grins, then lets out an extended, loudly vocal yawn.

"*Namaste*," I repeat—a traditional yogi benediction that means, loosely translated, "The universal in me salutes the universal in you."

—*Catherine Grow*

Best Quail Dog in the Ozarks

Dad always named his bird dogs "Lucille." He always owned black and white, female English setters for one really good reason.

"She dogs are smarter than males and easier to train," he would say. And my mother would giggle every time.

Dad and Uncle Ira loved to hunt quail. They were two of the best shots in the county and usually brought home a limit of birds. What they were most competitive about was who had the best bird dog.

Uncle Ira owned pointers and crossbreeds that were always males. As best I could figure, he did it only to be different. He always named his dogs "Hopalong," after a favorite cowboy character he listened to on the radio when he was a kid. He called them "Hop" for short. Anytime my dad talked about

Uncle Ira's dogs, the words "hardheaded" and "long-ranging" came into play.

There was a good reason why we had some of the best quail hunting in the Ozark Mountains. Quail primarily eat grain and acorns and require water close to where a covey would range, and we had a plentiful supply of everything, including an abundance of ponds, rivers, and lakes. Farmers planted a lot of corn and would leave a few rows along the edge of their fields for quail to eat. There were wooded areas filled with oak trees that shed a plentiful crop of acorns. Brush and blackberry vines that matted the fencerows provided shelter from predators and winter storms. Most all of our country was a quail paradise.

Shotguns and bird dogs were traded as frequently as a rooster in a barnyard switches hens. The ideal bird dog has a nose that can pick up a scent and track down birds even if they were on the run. It's a dog that will root around in a thicket or splash into the water after a cripple or a kill, honor another dog on point, never get so close as to flush the birds, and always obey a master's command. It's a dog with a soft mouth that can retrieve a bird without ruffling a feather.

I learned early on that even normally sane and generally responsible men would go to great lengths to find a good dog. It was the quest to own the best bird dog in the county that drove Uncle Ira to the extreme and caused his downfall on more than one occasion. Uncle Ira was smart as a whip in most ways, but when it came to having bird-dog–swappin' sense, Dad said he seemed to have little to none.

Quail are not easy to hit, and most who hunted them for meat used a Browning automatic 12-gauge shotgun with improved cylinder bore so the shot pattern would be widespread. Dad and Uncle Ira took pride in sporting Model 42, Winchester pump 410-gauges with a modified bore. Anyone who could bag a limit of quail with a small gauge shotgun had to be quick on the uptake and dead on their fluttering prey when they pulled the trigger.

"Time for breakfast!" Mom yelled up the stairs.

"Be right down!" I shouted back.

I sat on the edge of the bed and looked out the window at the pale winter sun rising above the rooftop of the corncrib, a gray weathered building my grandfather had built from hand-hewn logs in the early 1900s. A layer of frost covering the rusted tin roof sparkled like a million tiny diamonds. I stared at the gate that led into the barn lot and remembered how on another cold winter day, at the urging of my friend Iver, I'd tried to lick a piece of ice off of the metal latch and my tongue got stuck. I'd jerked my head back when I realized I was trapped, leaving soft pink skin on the gate. My tongue was so raw that for two weeks nourishment had to come from milk sucked through a straw. I was six years old at the time; I was eight now and not as easy to fool.

I was so excited about hunting with Dad and Uncle Ira on opening day of quail season that I had slept fitfully during the night. My job was to carry dead birds and to keep a close eye on where the singles set down after a covey was flushed. I was anxious to see Uncle Ira's new bird dog work the field. He claimed it was one of the best dogs in the county, even though it was a crossbreed and looked a bit different. I jumped out of bed to dress for a cold winter day: two pairs of socks, insulated long johns, and my tan hunting pants with a double layer of cloth that covered the front of my legs to protect me from the thorn bushes.

"What are you doing, Tommy?" Dad yelled. "Ira's ready to hit the field and show off his new bird dog."

"Be right down," I said as I tied my boots. Looking at myself in the mirror, I ran my fingers through my long, wavy brown hair, put on a bright orange hunting cap, and headed for the stairs.

When I walked into the kitchen, Dad and Uncle Ira were already eating and having a conversation about who owned the best bird dog of all time. It was more of the same old lingo about pointing, backing, and retrieving birds.

"So you've got another new dog," Dad said to Uncle Ira as he looked at me and winked. He forked a piece of gravy-covered ham into his mouth and washed it down with a swig of black coffee.

"Hold your comments until you see him hunt. He's a Weimaraner and Brittany spaniel mix. Doesn't look like your average, run-of-the-mill dog."

Uncle Ira saying that made Dad laugh. "I can hardly wait to see the critter. You've named him 'Hopalong,' as usual, I'd guess?"

"Nope. Haven't named him anything yet. I figured I'd let Tommy come up with a name."

In preparation for our exposure to his new dog, Uncle Ira could not resist giving us a bit more description. "Like I said, the dog looks out of the ordinary. Got short legs; a long body; thick, reddish-brown and white fur." When Dad looked at me and grinned, Ira said, "Proof's in the pudding. Wait 'til you see the dog hunt before rendering judgment."

"Did you know the fella who owned the dog?" Dad asked.

Uncle Ira shook his head back and forth as he pushed away from the table. "Like I said, the hunt will tell the story."

As we walked across the yard toward Uncle Ira's brand new red 1948 Chevy pickup, Dad saw Uncle Ira's new dog bouncing up and down on the seat and laughed. When I got a close look, I laughed as well. Uncle Ira's description could only conjure up a fraction of the way the dog looked.

We put Dad's dog Lucille and Ira's newfound treasure in the bed of the pickup truck and headed for the field.

Dad's only question along the way was if Uncle Ira had seen the dog hunt before he forked over the money. There was no answer.

When we arrived at the field to hunt and got out of the cab, the dogs jumped from the truck bed onto the ground. Uncle Ira's new dog made a beeline for the fence row, jumped a rabbit, and disappeared as he chased it into the woods.

"I didn't know good bird dogs would mess with rabbits," Dad said with a smile.

Uncle Ira looked the other way and shook his head. "I think I know what to name your new dog," I said, remembering a character in a comic book I had recently read. "How about 'Zig Zag.' We'll call him 'Zig' for short."

At that point, I could have said we should name the little fella "the devil," and Uncle Ira could not have cared less.

We walked in silence along the edge of the corn-field for a ways until Lucille went on point. As we stepped behind her, Zig came out of nowhere, ran past, and flushed the covey of birds. Uncle Ira took a wild shot and knocked a bird down. When it hit the ground, Zig grabbed the bird and started to chew like it was his supper.

Uncle Ira yelled and ran after Zig. Once again, the dog disappeared into the woods. By now, Zig was no longer at the top of Uncle Ira's "best bird dog in the county" list for sure.

As we continued the hunt, Zig appeared again at the end of the cornfield, only this time he was dragging something black toward us. Too big to be a crow; no white strip, so couldn't be a skunk. As we watched, the wind blew up a terrible smell, like a mixture of rotten eggs and sour milk. When he got close enough, his find was obvious.

"Looks like your dog's found himself a dead buz-zard," Dad said.

"What's that crawling on its feather?" I asked as I cocked my head to one side.

"That's maggots, Son," Dad said as he pinched his nose and walked away.

Uncle Ira hurried over and snapped a leash on Zig's collar, led him back to the truck, and shut him up inside the cab. Dad and I agreed there was no need to say nary another word about Zig not being much good as a bird dog. When Ira joined us again, Dad struck up a conversation about how much he liked Ira's new truck, and I said red was my favorite color.

As we hunted the rest of the field, Lucille pointed a couple of coveys. Dad and Uncle Ira got a half-dozen birds each, and we called it a day.

As we walked toward the truck as the sun shone brightly overhead, I noticed the cab looked like it was filled with spider webs. Uncle Ira noticed it right then too. He took off in a run, yelling, "What have you done?" Zig had ripped the headliner out of Uncle Ira's brand new truck, and the cotton strings were hanging down from the top of the cab.

To make a long story short, Dad told Uncle Ira he would give him the pick of the litter next time Lucille had pups as a Christmas present. He would also help him train the dog so Uncle Ira could stop searching all over the county for a better bird dog.

As it turned out, Dad's daughter Jeannie adopted Zig and taught him all kinds of tricks, including standing on his hind legs and turning in a circle while howling a song that sounded a lot like a low growling version of "Jingle Bells."

—Rolland Love

Sheriff Bean and His Posse

Bean has rules. When you tip the scales at only eight pounds, as Bean does, and you're shorter than the cats that live with you, you've got to do something. So you make rules and back them up with lots of noise.

Until a few months ago, Bean belonged to my friend. But when her son developed an allergy to him, Bean was welcomed into my family. I wasn't sure how a feisty six-year-old Chihuahua would fit in with my two cats and my number one dog, Annie, but I knew we'd make it work.

Bean considers my cats to be an inferior species, kind of like big hairy rats, only more crude and with fewer manners. Before coming to live here, he had little experience with them. He clearly thinks they need etiquette lessons and he's just the guy to teach them. That's why he developed most of his rules. It's also how he earned his nickname, "The Sheriff."

Sheriff Bean's rules range from helpful to annoying to amusing. Soon after moving in, he discovered that cats like to scratch the furniture, because they are, well, cats. They have a lovely scratching post, which they studiously ignore. Bean quickly realized that furniture scratching is against my rules, so he jumped right on that bandwagon. If a paw so much as stretches in the direction of the sofa, Bean is instantly on the case, snarling and threatening, his head turned slightly sideways but his eyes focused on the offender. So far, he hasn't had to back up his menacing warning with further action. But if Bean has anything to say about it, and he does, furniture scratching will not be tolerated. The cats usually turn in mid-scratch to give him the "say what?" look. But they stop. For that, I appreciate Bean's rule.

I'm less appreciative of his rules about nocturnal cat prowling. The rule is, once Bean goes to sleep for the night, you don't disturb him. I have the same rule for myself, but nobody really cares. If a cat wants to poke around the kitchen in search of a snack, I can sleep through it. Not Bean. With those megaphone-style ears of his, he hears the slightest paw-fall and shoots out of bed in a fierce barking frenzy. To make it worse, his noise wakes Annie, who joins in the 3:00 A.M. bark fest.

After my heart stops pounding and I verify that the only house prowler is a resident feline, I crawl back under the blankets, but too soon. Because, by then, Bean and Annie have decided that, since they're up anyway, a snack sounds pretty good. The two of them lobby me until, in sleepy desperation, I give in. Naturally, the canines have their own perspectives on these pre-dawn fiestas. When the alarm sounds and I get up to spend a day working at my nearby computer, they will feign sleep and refuse to budge from their comfy beds for hours to come.

Here's another Bean rule: He's instituted a no-fly zone for Annie and the cats. Occasionally, they fail to give him wide enough berth when he has a special treat, like a milk bone, known to Bean as a "boney." Whether he's eating it or burying it in the couch, Annie and the cats are supposed to respect his space whenever a boney is present. Otherwise, he'll take on all comers, baring his teeth as if asking, "You wanna piece o' me?" When boneys are involved, he adds a special sound that is neither a growl nor a bark but more like a chewing-in-progress sound, something like *muh-yah, muh-myah, myh-myah!* Only Bean knows what it really means. Of course, as he's delivering his fierce invective (from his well-known lecture series, entitled "Bean's Personal Space 101" or "Paws Off My Boney!"), his wagging tail belies his real feelings. That is, the undeniable truth among beast and man that the desirability of an object rises in direct proportion to how many other beings want it.

Since my house is not a ranch where dogs are expected to work for their meals, Bean came here to live a life of doggy leisure, like most pets. On chilly days he takes long naps tucked deep inside the small blanket, which he somehow manipulates into the shape of a bean burrito. His loud snoring provides the "music" while I work at my computer. Even so, with so many rules to enforce, it's clear that he is, in fact, a working dog. From inside his burrito he keeps watch over my household and those conniving cats. He's deeply suspicious of all passersby and assumes they are up to no good. Astute dog that he is, Bean is not even slightly fooled by that guy in the postal uniform who ventures a little too close to the house every afternoon.

I tell you all of this so that you'll get the picture: Bean has rules. And he means business about enforcing them. The cats shall not scratch the furniture. Neither shall they wake him, lest they incur the loud and obnoxious wrath of Bean. And heaven help the creature who gets too close to his boneys. Though I call him the Sheriff, the Drill Sergeant would work equally well. However, like real sheriffs and real drill sergeants, Bean has his Achilles heel.

Those who know Bean well know that he is a hypocrite. In other words, he has his price. Like the time my mom-cat Gracie decided she'd had enough of his grandstanding. Actually, she was just being who she is, a nurturer. One evening Bean had fallen asleep on my lap while I was reading on the couch. He was in Bean-heaven, sleeping away and making his usual assortment of sleep noises . . . until Gracie decided there was probably room on my lap for her too, if she sort of halfway lay on top of Bean. Before Gracie had set a single paw on me, Bean sprang to life, giving her heck for the intrusion. I could practically hear him order in a gravelly voice, "Drop to the floor, recruit! One hundred push-ups the hard way!" But Gracie remained unimpressed. She'd raised a rowdy brood of kittens, so Bean was no challenge.

That's when the unthinkable happened. Gracie put one paw on Bean's belly and pushed him back down on my lap. Then, like any good nurturer, she gave him a good belly washing. I thought he smelled pretty clean, but I guess Gracie didn't, because she washed and washed. At first Bean thrashed about, snarling and humiliated that an inferior beast had pinned him and was now questioning his personal hygiene. But soon the thrashing lost intensity. It was like watching an angry surgical patient succumb to the anesthesia, quickly going from hostile to feeling-no-pain euphoria. The growls were soon replaced with a noise that resembled an endless stream of *uh-uh-uh-uh-uh-uh*. And soon he was snoring again, even smiling.

It's a good thing Bean had a nice long sleep after that. Because he would've been even more embarrassed had he known that, after his belly was clean enough for her, Gracie used him for a pillow and took her own nap.

Since that day, there has not been a repeat of the belly-washing episode or anything like it. Maybe Gracie, in her gentle, nurturing way, needed to show Bean that she could take him if she had to. Or maybe she just wanted to expose him for the push-over he is. I prefer to think she was just illustrating the universal principle that, in spite of all the bluster from males like Bean, the toughest beings in the world are still the moms.

In many ways, Bean and Gracie are like a married couple. He continues to be the feisty, yappy sheriff who enforces his rules with bluster. And most of the time, Gracie obeys Bean's rules just because she's a gentle soul and a peacekeeper at heart. But now and then when they meet in the hall, a sideways glance passes between them that indicates they both know how it really is. Bean has his rules. And Gracie allows him to have them.

—Teresa Ambord

Not a Dog Lover

I do not love dogs. Or rather, I do not love dog-owners—especially the way they talk to and about their dogs, permit their pets access to my crotch ("He's just being friendly"), and kiss their four-legged darlings on the lips. Yuk! I know one woman who threw a doggy party, where she "married" her pooch. Dog owners are nuts.

But then, Casey entered my life. I had bribed my children to move to a new neighborhood with the promise of a dog. And after seeing my husband Ron stop the car on an overseas trip to play with a particularly beautiful hound that was rare in the United States, I knew what breed that canine should be. I, of course, would have nothing to do with it. I had grown up with a dog, wasn't afraid of dogs, just not interested, thank you.

At Ron's big birthday party, one of those milestone events ending with a zero and attended by people numbering in the two zeros, our friend Frank waited in the next room with a Rhodesian Ridgeback puppy already weighing twenty-five pounds. On cue, the music stopped and the M.C. started barking some poetry. Minutes later, the puppy nestled in my dropped-jawed husband's arms. He thought he'd been handed a dachshund.

"It's as if you removed your diaphragm and didn't tell me," he bristled under his breath at the same moment he bent his head and planted a kiss on the dog's head. "I can't believe you did this to me." He flashed me an angry glance as his lips again brushed the crown of short, brown puppy fur.

Smiling, I relaxed back in my seat.

Ron discovered that this dog had legs, after all, and tears filled his eyes.

"You're supposed to kiss me a 'thank you,'" I mumbled, aware of the hundreds of eyes watching the scene. But Ron was too busy kissing the dog and stroking the ridge of short hair growing peculiarly upward along the spine before ending in a perfect heart made from twin cowlicks.

For the next thirteen years, Casey was the friendly rival for my husband's affection. But she and I worked out our respective roles: She would accompany him on his long daily walks that disagreed with my back. She would yodel with him whilst I remained too self-conscious to belt my heart out. She would pee in the woods with him with no concern for poison ivy.

In summer, she strutted gracefully like a proud horse race. In winter, when forced to wear a heavy sweater to go outdoors, she kept her head down in embarrassment. I appreciated the fact that she never barked, but I sometimes wished she had been bred to fetch the newspaper rather than to clear our New York suburb of lions.

Soon, Casey and I forgot that she was a dog. Nobody ever told her that, and I, well, I treated her like one of my children. And she knew I was her mommy. When a vicious dog bit her flank, she glided over silently and presented her backside to me for medical care. When on vacation once, as I came upon her tethered by a rope to some stranger, her eyes begged me to rescue her. She kept me company in the long months I worked on each of my novels, her one-hundred-and-twenty pound bulk under my desk, a willing leg rest. Before long, I began spelling out words such as "bed," "east" (sounds like "eat"), and "Lady" (her playmate), or she'd retire with great sadness to bed or run excitedly to her bowl or the door. Driving a car, I would point out a cow or a pigeon to

Casey as I would to a three-year-old child. Her wise glance followed the subjects.

What did I say about dog owners? I became just as nutty!

Exactly a year to the day that, sobbing, we held the old and very ill Casey while the veterinarian put her out of her misery, Ron and I were in the Galapagos Islands. One afternoon, exhausted from a snorkeling excursion, we collapsed on the beach and, taking the cue from the hundreds of sea lions soaking up the sun all along the shoreline, we dropped our towels on the sand and stretched out.

Sea lions and people did not bother each other in these protected grounds. More than unafraid of us two-legged animals, they were oblivious to our presence. And visitors would no more approach them than they would the iguanas scattered about, whose sole interest focused on waiting for the cacti's sweet yellow flowers to drop into their open mouths.

"Look at that sea lion," Ron pointed at the two-hundred-fifty–pound female beached next to her giant mate, facing us. Her head rested on the sand. "She has Casey's face."

Yes, she did, I agreed, eyeing the beast from fifty feet away. The same pretty snout, the same short brown hair sleeked back, the same expressive dark eyes.

Ron sighed, as he had been doing often that year. "If Casey were here, she'd lie right between us and put her head on my shoulder."

Ninety seconds later, the female sea lion raised her head. She sniffed the air. Then she hefted her body. She began waddling toward us.

I was the obstacle in her line of advancement. I jumped to my feet, but it was too late to yank my towel, as the guest had just claimed it.

Ron did not move. The sea lion sniffed him, her whiskers tickling his neck, his ear, his cheek. He lay still. She sniffed some more. Then she placed her massive head on his shoulder.

I am still not a dog lover. But Casey was not a dog.

—*Talia Carner*

Bear's Boys

I sat down on my neighbor's living room floor.
"Are you ready?" she asked.

"I'm ready!"

She opened the back door slowly, and six white, furry, smushed-nosed puppies piled in the back door. While one leaped for my nose, another attacked my ears. There were happy puppy tails everywhere, each one vying for my attention as I laughed and tried to protect my face.

"How will I choose?" I asked hopelessly.

Then, in the midst of all that havoc, one lone puppy laid down on my lap. He let the others jump and play at will, but this puppy simply lay down as if to say he had found his home.

"Never mind." I smiled at the calm puppy. "I found him."

And I took him home to my sons.

Marsh and Ryan were typical boys. They ran, played baseball, and rode their bikes to school. After the day I brought the puppy—which they christened "Bear"—home from his litter, it was rare to find the boys without him.

Whether the boys were sleeping or lying on their bellies in front of the TV, Bear was always there. He chased balls when they played baseball, and he ran through the fields beside them when they played cops and robbers. Best of all, as the boys grew older and bolder, Bear protected them fiercely.

During my divorce, Bear comforted the boys with his steady presence. The day we left the family home and moved into a townhouse, I let the boys go explore the new neighborhood, but I kept Bear in the house.

"We don't want him to get lost," I explained to the boys. "We'll let him get used to the house first, and then you guys can take him out on leash until he knows where home is. Alright?"

While the boys and Bear were clearly unhappy with my decision, Bear stayed with me while I unpacked and the boys went outside with a football in their hands. I could hear them laughing and talking as they passed the football back and forth, so I called Bear and we went upstairs to unpack the bedrooms.

It was not long, though, before I realized I could no longer hear my sons. I went outside, carefully shutting Bear in the house, and called their names.

I could hear Bear inside the house scratching at the door and whimpering, but I ignored him and kept calling the boys. I walked all the way around the house yelling their names as loud as I could, but I got no response.

I began to panic. They were only seven and nine years old. My imagination began to invade my good sense. I had horrible thoughts of some maniac enticing my boys into a car or a nasty neighbor I had yet to meet luring them into his home. My heart raced faster and fear crept into my voice as I yelled louder, again and again. Eventually, I ran back into the house and picked up the phone to call 9-1-1.

It was then, with Bear leaning his body against my leg and peering up into my eyes, that I remembered a trick my mother would use when she wanted my sisters and me to come home. I hung up the phone.

"You can find them, can't you, boy?" I said to Bear as I reached down to scratch behind his ears.

I found paper and pen in the box labeled "desk," and I simply wrote, "Boys, come home."

I dug a safety pin out of my sewing basket and hooked the paper to Bear's collar, all the while talking to the boy's faithful companion as if he were human. "You need to go find them, boy. Bring them home to me, alright?"

When the note was securely fastened, I walked to the front door and opened it. Bear looked at me expectantly.

"Go get them! Go find your boys."

I watched as he raced out the door and sped away.

The only thing I could do was stand there and pray. I shut the door and tried to remain calm. Tears filled my eyes; I blinked them back. I reasoned I'd give Bear fifteen minutes before I would call the police. I looked at the clock and began to mark time.

To give myself something to do, I pulled ice cubes out of the tray and fixed a glass of ice water. I looked into the refrigerator and saw two apples, glad that the boys would have something to snack on when they came home.

I looked at the clock and took a deep breath. It had been only five minutes; I could wait ten more. As the minutes ticked by, I fluctuated between being angry with the boys for scaring me to being terrified something horrible had befallen them.

Then my miracle happened.

I heard voices. Boy voices.

I ran to the door and threw it open. Across the yard I could see my sons happily running toward home with Bear yipping at their heels. I ran into the yard and embraced them both at the same time. Then I bent to pick up our small, furry Sherlock Holmes. "Where were they, Bear? Where did you find them?"

"We found a creek just up over that hill, Mom!"

"And we were trying to catch the fish with our bare hands . . ."

"And then a weird thing happened . . ."

His brother took over, "Bear showed up, and he had a note on his collar!"

Marsh finished, "It said, 'Boys, come home.' How did you know he'd find us, Mom?"

"Yeah! How did you know?"

I snuggled my nose into Bear's furry neck and lifted thankful eyes to my sons. "Bear will always find you no matter where you go, don't you know that?" I asked.

And through the years, Bear proved that loyalty time and again. He protected them and he guarded them. When the boys were out of my sight, I always took comfort in knowing their dog was with them. Before I could blink, Ryan had graduated and was living a scant mile away in a house of his own. Bear waited at home. In his old age, he slept most of the time, but he was always hopeful for one of his boys' frequent visits.

One Friday, a day I remember as if it were yesterday, I'd just started working on a quilt when Bear became unnaturally fretful. Marsh was due home from college, but there was something about Bear's anxious whimpering that worried me.

Ryan stopped by for a visit, and as he walked in the door, Bear, blinded in his old age, immediately put his nose in the air. He could tell one of the boys was in the house by his scent alone. He quickly put his nose to the ground and made a beeline for Ryan's feet.

"He's been acting anxious all day, Ryan. I don't know what's wrong."

Ryan sat on the floor and pulled the ancient dog, by then 126 dog-years-old, into his lap.

"What's the matter, old boy? Are you okay?"

Ryan spent the next hour or so talking with me, all the while holding Bear in his lap and scratching him behind the ears. Soon Bear calmed down and eventually went back to sleep. Even as Ryan rose to leave and laid the dog on his sleeping rug, Bear seemed calmer than he had been all day.

I hugged Ryan goodbye and went back to my quilt.

It wasn't long, however, before the furry white nose went back into the air and good old Bear shuffled over to lay his head on my foot once again.

For the next few hours, Bear would occasionally lift his head, sniff the air, and whimper. I would scratch him behind the ears and he would lie back down, but his clouded eyes remained opened, as if sightlessly watching.

It was four o'clock when I heard the elderly Volkswagon pull into the driveway. Bear whimpered once again, but I reached down and patted his head.

"Hold on, old man. Your other boy just got home."

I left him lying on the kitchen floor, made my way out the front door, and hugged Marsh as he pulled his laundry out of the mouth of the old VW.

"You better go in the house, Marsh," I said as I took his laundry from him. "Bear has been really fretful today. Go say hello."

Marsh hugged me and let me have his bundle. Then he headed into the house.

I continued unpacking his car and carried his belongings to the porch. When I entered the living room, I found Marsh sitting in the rocking chair holding a calm and quiet Bear. I reached out and touched Marsh's shoulder. When Marsh raised his eyes to mine, I saw the tears falling freely down his cheeks.

"He's gone, Mom," Marsh said quietly. "When I came in, he lifted his nose and came right to me. I picked him up and sat down with him on my lap, then he took his last breath."

That's when it dawned on me. The wonderful old dog simply wanted to say goodbye to his boys. That was the reason he had been so anxious. Once he had seen them both one more time, he could go in peace.

The boys buried their trusted friend in our yard, and Bear's grave is still marked by a cross they made with their own hands. The cross is weathered and old, sitting slightly askew. But when my boys—now grown men with families of their own—see the old cross, they remember. They think of the white, furry, little dog chasing after their bicycles. They can still smell the scent of his fur as they called him to bed at night. They remember how Bear jumped like a yo-yo trying to lick their faces as they arrived home from school. They recall the day their trusted dog found them at the stream. And they smile.

—Lori Bottoms

Miss Stinky: Queen for a Day

Miss Stinky had a real name—Goldy, I believe it was, due to her coloring, golden, like the retriever. But her physique was pure hippo. She had the waistline of a Southern belle who's had a few too many hush puppies and moon pies. She also had the ripe aroma of a dog who loved the water and all the creatures in it—notably the fish and especially the dead ones. I called her Miss Stinky from day one, when she showed up on Preston Island, Alabama, and declared it home.

Back in those days, dogs of all kinds would show up following First Monday, the monthly swap meet on the town square. Hunting dogs, along with pigs and chickens and whatever else ended up in the back of pickups, were bought and sold by men in dusty overalls and boots. Dogs who didn't find a home were turned loose out on the highway, to eke out a living on their own or to finagle their way into the cushy life of a housedog. Most of them never made it past that first week on their own. But Miss Stinky was a plucky gal—the kind of little lady who takes lemons and turns them into lemon-frosted dog biscuits.

The first thing you noticed about Miss Stinky—after the smell, which assaulted you whenever you got within a stone's throw—was her smile. And don't say that dogs don't smile, because they do. I've seen it. After she found her way to Preston Island, she was nothing but smiles, because she had landed in dog heaven and she knew it.

Strictly speaking, Preston Island is more of a landing pad in the Tennessee River than an island. But for people and dogs, it's a little like heaven. There is only one road around the island, so traffic is just the occasional pickup truck or golf cart—neighbors just puttering by with a wave. Most of the houses have lake access right outside the front door, and dogs roam freely—swimming, running, and generally whooping it up, as only dogs can do. Those country dogs would scoff at my current canine, a city dog who goes to doggie daycare to socialize and to a fenced-in dog park to run. There are no fences on Preston Island.

Miss Stinky was an island dog. She belonged to no one and yet to everyone. I hardly remember a time when she wasn't the queen of the island, the welcoming committee, the cruise director, and the band leader. She patrolled the island like a beneficent monarch visiting her subjects. And always, she was a Southern lady, hospitable to the core.

In the mornings I would go running, and Miss Stinky would join me at a vigorous waddle. We were up at dawn, with the sunrise sparkling on the water and the towering pine trees scenting the cool morning air, she carrying her stick, and me with my water bottle. As we passed house after house, we would pick up one dog, then another dog and another, until I was like the Pied Piper of Preston Island with a pack of ten dogs running with me. There was no squabbling, just a pack of happy dogs, with Miss Stinky in the lead, smiling, dripping wet from a swim, and nice and fishy from a good roll in something dead. Dead things were her specialty.

With a Southerner's generosity, she always arrived bearing presents—sticks, leaves, or just a big wad of mud, presented with a smile. It's the thought that counts.

Despite the fact that she had no official home, she was well cared for. In fact, the waddle in her gait and her generously padded midsection was evidence of her well-being. She never lacked for food. When she needed to go to the vet, she was escorted. When it was particularly cold outside, there was always a warm blanket in a heated spot for her. She was loved by many and indebted to none.

Perhaps, like Scarlett O'Hara, she never forgot the hard years. As God was her witness, she would never be hungry again—and by God, she was not. She laid in that store of belly fat in case the lean years happened to return. Thankfully, they never did, but no doubt she'd had a few dark years in her past—years when she became a mother, a big red dog in the rural South with no home and puppies to nurse. No food. Cold nights. Fear. I never asked and she never told. Once she got to Preston Island, she never looked back—and the only hint of her previous trials was the well-stocked pantry she kept around her middle. After she adopted the island, life was pure unadulterated joy punctuated with snacks.

As a Southern belle—albeit one with mud, twigs, and fish scales sticking out of her fur and the pungent aroma of dead lake creatures wafting around her at all times—it was only fitting that Miss Stinky enter a beauty pageant. This was decreed, and all were in favor. The doing of it was another matter, however. Imagine 100 pounds of wet fishy dog, matted fur, years of crusted whooziwhatsits in her coat and goodness only knows what all—well, the cleanup was a job. But in the end, Miss Stinky—Goldy, I mean—was shampooed, blow-dried, brushed, and coiffed into perfection. Her chestnut coat gleamed, and she was bestowed with the customary beauty pageant sash that read, "Miss Preston Island."

Then she was driven to the big city—or the smallish local town, as it were—and had her 15 seconds of fame up there on the stage. Afterward, she had her portrait taken, with the blue velvet backdrop and everything. I still have that picture, framed. And in it, she is still smiling that big, fish-eating grin.

It's a truism that happiness in this world is fleeting. I often think of Miss Stinky and her happy-go-lucky ways—her lack of attachment, her joy in the moment. I guess all dogs are like that, but some nestle into your heart a little more than others.

Miss Stinky taught me—above all—to roll around in that dead fish today because it might be gone tomorrow. To never hesitate to get your paws dirty. To keep the pantry stocked, to always smile for the camera, and to keep playing, no matter how deep the mud.

—Elizabeth Brewster

Under the Hemlock Tree

Hector had free run of the countryside. Chaining him was egregious cruelty, he thought. So did I. Because I lived in a cabin out in the woods with no road to it and no close neighbors, I felt safe letting Hector run free. When he finished his woodland explorations, he curled up in a favorite resting spot under a hemlock tree—moss-covered, comfortable, safe, and near me. With this freedom to come and go at will, Hector led a happy life.

September came, glorious but nippy. The breath of August had barely fled when I relented and let Hector inside for a bit. He stretched out on the strip of linoleum between my carpet and kitchen counter. Hector well knew the carpet was forbidden territory. While I sat in front of the fire with my nose in a book, he lay, the epitome of innocence. Almost imperceptibly, he inched forward—forepaws, muzzle, head. How could he be accused of disobeying? When I looked up, half of Hector's body rested on the carpet.

"Hector. Off the carpet!"

Hector groaned and moved back to the linoleum. I went to him, stroked his silky head, told him what a fine fellow he was, and returned to my book. When my head nodded, I got up and called to Hector. "Okay, fellow, out you go." I watched as Hector headed for the hemlock tree, then I climbed the ladder to my loft bedroom.

Dawn hadn't yet stretched and yawned when I heard Hector banging his food dish. The morning was cold; my bed was warm. I burrowed under blankets and continued sleeping until tyrannical dictates against slothfulness forced me out of bed around eight. I clambered down the ladder from my loft, put coffee on, and took food out to Hector.

"Hector, breakfast. Come."

I wasn't alarmed when Hector didn't bound up. He'd be around soon. I left his food under the hemlock tree and went about my morning chores, giving Hector hardly a thought. That afternoon, I gathered my berry buckets, slipped on my backpack, and called for Hector. A tick of alarm stirred when I noticed Hector's breakfast was still in his dish.

I scrambled down the side of the gravel pit, crossed over to the railroad track, and headed for a cottonwood stand across Glacier Creek. As I walked, I called for Hector. My heart surged when a flash of white waved over the marsh on the far side of the railroad bridge. *There he is. There's Hector.*

"Here, Hector, here," I yelled as I ran toward the marsh.

The flash of white—a seagull—flew away.

Dispirited, I plunged into a cottonwood stand by Glacier Creek to search for high bush cranberries. My buckets filled quickly with panicles of red berries, but this bounty gave me no pleasure. I wanted Hector along, darting through underbrush, sniffing and panting with doggie busyness.

When my containers were full, I headed home, hurrying to the top of the gravel pit, expecting to find Hector trotting up the trail, wagging a happy greeting. As I approached my cabin, I stretched my eyes, searching for Hector. No Hector appeared.

Where is that dog?

I deposited my berries and ran through the woods. "Hector. Here, Hector."

My calls echoed through the forest. A red squirrel chirred. A warbler rustled azalea leaves. A branch snapped back in my face. Rubbing the sting, I dashed on, but I saw no flash of white. I saw no Hector.

I turned around and trudged toward my cabin, fear squeezing my heart. As I turned into the yard, my eyes flew to the hemlock tree. Empty shadows and a full food dish mocked me. By this time, dusk darkened the woods. I ate, then trudged woodland paths querying neighbors. None, no one, had seen Hector.

Dispirited, I scrambled down the gravel pit to my car and drove to the Double Musky. Lively concertina music met my ears as I dragged myself through the parking lot. Inside, polkaing couples whooped it up, pounding the dance floor until it shook. My sodden spirits weighted me as I shouldered through the crowd, inquiring.

"No."

"Nope."

"No, haven't seen him."

It was after midnight when I walked the moonlit path to my cabin. Stark and still, hemlock shadows spiked the trail, piercing me with emptiness.

In my loft bed, I tossed. Agonized thoughts stampeded my mind. *Hector would come home if he could. Did someone take him? A moose kick him? A car hit him? A bear attack him? Is he lying somewhere, injured and helpless?*

Scraps of sleep came, with fitful dreams in which I struggled toward Hector, trying to reach him—trying, trying—trying in vain.

At first light, I arose and checked Hector's spot under the hemlock tree. Empty. Futile though I knew it was, I stepped outside and split the air with calls for Hector.

I skipped breakfast, hiked to my car, and drove the Seward Highway. Dreading to look, I scanned ditches. I drove north, I drove south, calling, calling. No live Hector came bounding. No dead Hector lay among the cow parsnips.

Back at my cabin, a vole crawled inside Hector's battered food dish, taking advantage of a free meal. I dumped the food behind my cabin for wild foragers and took another sweep through the woods. Futile shouts faded in the forest.

On Sunday, I abandoned my search and went hiking with friends. A week earlier, we'd planned the hike, along with a post-hike meal at my cabin. I submerged my despondency, intending to slug my way through the day.

After the hike, as we approached my cabin, my heart lurched. A still, white mound lay at my doorstep. Dreading what I would find, I approached the heap and found a sack, lumpy and still. I steeled myself and pulled the drawstring.

Inside were four humpies (pink salmon), black and slimy. A note was slipped beneath the sack. I pulled it out. "Thought Hector would like these," it said.

I blinked and swallowed. Too late. Too late. Hector would have loved them.

I ushered my guests inside and hid my leaden heart while we sipped wine, ate chili, and talked. Around 1:00 A.M., my guests left. I climbed to my loft and, with the help of the wine, slept—sad but resigned.

Monday morning, I didn't bother looking outside. Hector was gone. I dragged through a joyless breakfast that sat heavy in my stomach. After eating, I brushed crumbs from the counter into my hand and took them outside for the birds. Out of habit, I looked under the hemlock tree.

My heart leapt. I flew down the steps. There under the hemlock tree lay Hector.

"Hector! Hector!" I cried.

Hector didn't move. He didn't wag his tail. But he lifted his head and made a feeble effort to greet me.

I ran inside for Hector's favorite food, filled his dog dish, and, nearly tripping in my haste, set it in a spot of sun near him. Whining, Hector struggled but couldn't rise. He yelped when I lifted him, then, arched and stiff, made his painful way to the dish. Love and relief washed over me as I sat on my railroad-tie steps and watched Hector bolt the food as though he hadn't eaten for three days—which, probably, he hadn't.

After Hector finished eating, I examined him. One leg was skinned, but it was the other leg he favored. A swelling bulged at the base of his tail. Hector yipped when I touched it, but praise the heavens, he was back!

I wanted to rush Hector to the vet right away, but it was Labor Day; I had to wait. That night, Hector slept on the carpet. I brought a sleeping bag down from the loft and slept beside him. Recognizing sympathy nearby, Hector whimpered throughout the night.

Tuesday morning, I drove my car as close to my cabin as I could get it. Hector was only five months old at the time, but still, he was heavy. Jeanne Waite, a friend who lived nearby, and I took turns carrying him the half-mile or so to my car. At the clinic in Anchorage, the vet X-rayed Hector.

"His pelvis is broken," the vet said. "He may have been hit by a car, rolled down an embankment, and scraped his leg in the fall."

With a broken pelvis, Hector had dragged himself home. It took him three days, but he made it. *What pluck, fine dog, fine hero dog,* I thought as I stroked him.

After Hector healed, I took him for walks down by the road. When a car came along, Hector stuck his tail between his legs and made a wide circuit away from it. That told the story. Hector had learned a hard lesson.

After that, I let Hector curl up on the carpet in front of the fire, right by me, where I could reach down and pet him. When I did, he licked his lips, swallowed, and wagged his tail. Plain as anything, he spoke: *Now, this is the way it ought to be.*

—*Betty Jo Goddard*

Gramps and the Harem

"What's the matter, Gramps?" I teased my eleven-year-old golden retriever, whose real name was Rhett.

He let out a tremendous sigh of exhaustion and then collapsed wearily onto the floor near my feet.

"Has Taylor worn you out again?"

He gave me such a woeful look that I had to laugh. Leaning over, I scratched his floppy ears. Although he seemed to appreciate my attention, he was simply too tired to wag his tail.

"That's okay, Rhett," I spoke softly as he drifted off to sleep. "Taylor is a handful."

And she was too. We'd had the new puppy for a year. During this time, the whole family had lost weight and gained muscles as we raced around trying to drain her excess energy. Taylor, a springer spaniel, black Labrador mix, was all action, all the time. Even with three walks a day and a backyard to pounce around in, she still had enough vim and vigor to keep old Rhett on his toes.

Mostly, that was a good thing. Taylor's vitality had undoubtedly added years to Rhett's life and a spirited spring to his step. Still, there were limits to his stamina. And Taylor loved to push them to the breaking point. But, beyond that, Rhett genuinely loved her to pieces; he positively doted on this feisty mutt and let her get away with everything. I am positive that no creature in this world has had a more adoring grandfather than Taylor.

Never was that more evident than on one warm summer day. Taylor was outside chasing some California lizards and Rhett was sound asleep. With the kids and my husband off on a Saturday adventure, I was curled up on the couch spellbound by the plot of a murder mystery. All was quiet and peaceful. Suddenly, a pack of hounds let out such a ruckus that I dropped my book and Rhett snapped to attention. Though it sounded like a dog shelter at dinner time, one deep, aggressive voice overruled the others.

"Perhaps the new neighbors have discovered Taylor."

The new neighbors consisted of a large boy dog and his three-girl harem.

From the window, I saw Taylor leap off our two-foot–high cement ledge and back away from the sturdy, six-foot wooden fence that divided our two yards. She was traveling as fast as her stocky little legs could carry her. A heartbeat later, she, wide-eyed and frightened, yammered to come in.

"What's the matter, Taylor?" I asked as I got up to open the door. "Are those new canines teaching you a lesson about who owns the neighborhood?"

Though I thought the situation was funny, Rhett was not amused. His expression was dour and dismayed. Before I'd reached the screened door to let the puppy in, Rhett had dragged his arthritic old hips from the floor and met Taylor at the door.

To my surprise, Rhett went charging out. He stood on the patio, his big nose busily sniffing his darling granddaughter for any tale-tail injustices. Finding none, he still gave me a look that seemed to say, "Can you believe the total arrogance of that dog next door? Imagine him saying such things to my baby!"

Sensing trouble, I, too, stepped out onto the porch. Watchfully, Taylor and I both stood by quietly as we waited for Rhett to assess the situation. First, he eyed the ledge separating the backyard from the fence. Though Taylor regularly hopped up and down it, Rhett, with his frail bones, hadn't attempted it in years.

We all took a deep breath. Then, in some silent doggy communication, Rhett motioned for Taylor to jump back up the ledge. Seconds later, he instructed her to go nearer the fence. Once in position, she glanced back at Rhett. He sniffed the air as his eyes darted along the length of the empty fence. He gave another canine signal, and Taylor began to bark ferociously. A heartbeat later, the air was filled with the raucous yapping and carrying on of the three female dogs. Another glance at Rhett, and Taylor kept up her terrible snarling.

Then we heard it: the boy next door came leaping and growling at the fence, his bark once again louder and more commanding than the others. Even I could tell he meant business—no mere female pup was going to challenge his authority!

I swear, Rhett smiled. This was the moment he'd been waiting for. Like a rusty, wobbly old rocket, he gathered his strength and literally launched himself, bounding and lurching, across the yard. I knew the exertion was painful for him. He didn't let out a sound until he'd hurled himself up on to the ledge and fired his entire ninety-pound bulk at that fence.

Again and again, he snapped and clawed at the wooden partition as if he were a rabid, fire-breathing coyote. Gallons of doggy adrenaline made him strong and steady. In all our years together, I'd never heard

Rhett sound so menacing, so ferocious, so totally animal. I was stunned speechless—and terrified that the fence would go down and all of those angry dogs would tumble into my yard.

Rhett and Taylor proved a formidable pair. But, make no mistake, the young stud and his all-girl team presented a pretty tough bunch as well. For a time, the six dogs parried and sparred. No doubt, the new kids on the block felt sure that the fence would protect them. Rhett, with his added years of wisdom, knew better. His relentless, forcefulness—his unshakable defense of his baby—eventually proved too much for the anchoring post. With a thunderous rip, it broke in half and left a gaping hole in the fence.

Now, Rhett struck like a gray-faced devil dog. He angled his head between the broken boards, baring his lethal fangs, his voice more determined than ever. Shocked by the unexpected meeting, the gang next door let out a communal yelp, then scattered across their own yard to the safety of their opened back door.

Rhett and Taylor held their stance until they heard the neighbor dogs go inside. Although Taylor, in her youthful exuberance, kept barking and bouncing around, anxious for one more crack at them, Rhett visibly shriveled. His shoulders sagged; his breath came in short, heavy pants. The poor old guy was totally done in.

Disappointed that the party was over, Taylor hopped off the ledge and quickly resumed her lizard chasing. Rhett, on the other hand, hobbled to its edge and looked down. Completely pooped, he turned his great brown eyes toward me. He was trembling; his ancient legs threatened to give out. Obviously, the long jump down would be disastrous.

"Wow, Rhett," I hurried over to him just as he began to topple over. I patted his head in admiration while I balanced his big body against my chest. "You are amazing."

Once more, he was too bedraggled to even wag his tail. I wrapped my arms around his shoulders and ribs to ease his descent to the ground. He licked my face in gratitude.

For the next few days, Taylor delighted in going up to the mended fence and barking her head off. Sometimes, from a distance, the harem would return her banter until a single woof from Rhett shut them all up. Never again did their mighty leader raise his voice to Taylor. And that deep sign of respect was all Gramps ever needed.

—*Loy Michael Cerf*

Cooking for Dogs

My wife grows impatient with me because I cook meals for our dogs.

These days, there are two. After an assortment of lost dogs, found dogs, and misfit dogs, we now live with a mismatched pair that matches my needs.

The old greyhound, his teeth worn or missing, demands little more than some peaceful time on his woolen rug as he comes to the end of his mortal run. The bulldog has chewed past puppy stage to reveal a sharp intelligence behind a snub nose and a wit complicated only by a willingness to debase herself by learning clownish tricks.

"A food slut," says my wife, laughing at the bulldog. She prefers cats. Cats tend themselves. Dogs demand attention.

I do not completely understand why I cook for these dogs. I am bemused by the element of emotional satisfaction mixed into the process.

Then there's the irony that I have grown to mimic my father. My father and I shared hazel eyes, a sardonic wit, and a love of animals. But we shared little else.

No, that's wrong. I once thought we shared a sense of my shortcomings. That was before I understood that a son's inadequacies and a father's failures cannot be found when a man bends down to clean stray grass and weeds away from a headstone.

Growing up, I was surrounded by animals, too much perhaps. It is only lately that I have begun to recognize the animal, rather than simply dealing with animals. It is only lately that I've tapped into the symbiotic link that flickered alight when man first tossed a bone to the beast lurking at the edge of the firelight.

As a youth, I would watch my father move among his animals. His posture no longer aloof and judgmental, he offered respect for their spirit and personalities.

Throughout his working life, my father managed staff and dealt with the public, and he was good at it. Popular, in fact. "A people person" you might say after meeting him. You would be wrong.

I think he liked individuals and mistrusted people. I think I am the same.

My father insisted on living away from the city where he worked. He insisted on owning land and animals. He insisted on keeping a horse too old to ride, dogs, cats, chickens, ducks, geese, turkeys, peafowl, and cattle. I know now he found silent, unexpressed comfort in caring for his animals.

I helped when I was a youngster, when there were cows to milk and calves to feed. When I grew older, he sold the dairy cows and moved to a smaller acreage. There, he watched over an economically unproductive menagerie of exotic chickens and ducks, a quarter horse or two, and a few calves.

My father walked among his animals, usually after supper, a cigarette smoldering at the corner of his mouth, carrying feed grain in discarded coffee cans. The evening's routine ended with my father brushing the horse while it ate alfalfa pellets or oats.

Now, I live in a city, but I cannot watch a horse without remembering my father. I live in a city, and I know more than a bit about Brangus and Beefmasters, Araucana, and Dominickers, but I have only dogs to remind me of the blood link to my people.

And today, my wife found weevils in the container where we store rice. She turned to toss it in the garbage.

"Wait," I said. "I'll rinse it and cook it for the dogs."

She sighed and glanced heavenward. My wife believes every product has a purpose, and dog food would not be manufactured if dogs were meant to eat other food.

I told her I do this because I like to cook and there is no other reason to cook. She prefers snacks to meals, and my appetite is minimal. The two boys we attempted to train as men have left to see what we made of them. So we need not cook. Our kitchen discussions center around who gets the majority of the not-quite-ripe bananas, proof again that we are divinely matched.

There are only dogs left to provide me purpose.

The boys and I once had a slapdash recipe for a dish we named "skillet chili," a rash concoction of ground beef, peppers, spices, and beans, tossed into my grandmother's deep cast-iron Griswold skillet. That's my culinary style. Together, we made Swiss steak, pork chops with sauerkraut, and stews.

Little of that is good for dogs. Nevertheless, I miss handling, preparing, and shaping that which I will eat. I find comfort in measuring, in applying knife to vegetables, in the taste and smell and texture of spices.

So I've gone to the dogs, not listening when my wife scoffs about time wasted, not listening when the dogs tell me they would be equally happy with raw ground beef directly from the package.

I remind the impatient dogs of the newspaper column by a veterinarian aptly named Fox. Dr. Fox believes tails should not be docked, cats should be kept indoors, and commercial pet foods should be used sparingly, if at all. He talks of flaxseed oil and fresh vegetables but never mentions the cost of PETA membership dues.

I wear leather and eat meat, but I suspect he's more right than radical when he rails against commercial dog food.

I know he's right about dogs eating vegetables. Do you dread the annual zucchini invasion? When that prolific squash threatens to overrun our summer garden, I put it on the canine menu.

Chop zucchini, boil it in chicken stock, and add eggs or corn or a few beans. I have cooked, the dogs have dinner, and there's no further talk of raw ground beef.

I rinse the rice. My wife has left to putter among her backyard flowers. I add a bouillon cube, some chopped garlic, and a bit of olive oil to the water as it begins to boil.

"Are you hungry?" I ask. The dogs hear my words, but they do not know it is the ghost of my father who questions them.

The bulldog listens carefully, eager to learn the progress of her meal. The old greyhound doesn't move from his rug until I toss in two or three eggs and add ice cubes to cool the mixture. The aroma wafts into the living room, and the greyhound stirs. The bulldog wiggles and hums.

I feel compelled to explain the process, because the dogs are perplexed by hot food. Enticed to drools and soft whimpers by the fragrance, they will pull back in confusion when I serve them something warm.

I divide the mixture. Obviously, they weren't listening carefully. Muzzles ease tentatively into the bowls as they sense the heat emanating from their dinner. Soon appetite outweighs the odd sensation, and they begin to gobble the food.

I am quiet, watching their posture, their eyes, the energy electrifying their frames. I watch them engorge themselves, and I try to narrow my focus, to shut out the noise and the light, to smell the wolf, to sense the primal.

A bulldog and a greyhound—utterly stylized creations wrought by man's desire for form and function—but wolf at heart, life-force in its most elemental, enduring form.

Prehistoric man tossed the bone, and the wolf snapped it up and retreated into the night. Other nights, other bones, and other wolves trailed the hunter-gatherers to scavenge, until one beast crept forward into the warmth of the fire and one man reached to touch him.

Is this why I take a few minutes to prepare food for these animals rather than prying open a can or shoveling kibble from a bag?

The dogs cannot tell me. Neither can my father. He is dead. Dogs know fear but are ignorant of that thing most fearful. I must rely upon myself. And I am young enough to know only that I dread my death, that my diminished appetite for food doesn't reflect my hunger for life. I shiver. "Good, huh?" I ask, seeking a way out of the shadow, a reconnection to the familiar.

The bulldog pays little attention, a flick of an ear and a glance upward, but perhaps the old greyhound scents my melancholy. He pauses and looks up, rice leaking from the space that once held his lower front teeth. His belly is filling, and, if there is disquietude, he senses it is receding, and that is good enough for a dog.

Is it good enough for me?

I suppose. I am content, for the moment, at least. Content with the work of my hands, which has brought comfort to two of God's creatures. Content with the amused affection my wife and I share for one another's foibles. Content with the knowledge that not every act needs a reason, nor every wound a bandage, nor every question an answer.

—*Gary Presley*

Gizmo's Way

Our fourteen-pound Shih Tzu, Gizmo, thought he was a big dog.

We didn't try to dissuade him. Surely, he could see it for himself. After all, we also owned another dog, a black Labrador. The next-door neighbor had a Lab too. And a variety of hefty dogs lived within howling distance. Despite all evidence to the contrary, though, Gizmo was convinced he was as large as the pack around him.

Somewhere between toddling into our lives as a puppy to the feisty grown male he'd become, we should have tried to show him the truth. But would he have recognized his reflection? Would he have known he was the long-haired, white-coated dog in the mirror with the large swathes of sorrel brown across his back? Had he seen himself with his own big buggy eyes, would he have realized that curiously small body as his own?

Even if he did, I doubt we could have persuaded him that he was not ninety pounds plus. Certainly, we could never convince him that his teeth could barely puncture a cucumber, let alone the thick neck of a dog three times his size. So we saw no harm in letting him believe he was top dog of the block. He treated shepherds and rottweilers equally, warning them off with a snarl. Gizmo considered this his job and always put in a good day's work.

In late summer of 2002, we moved. It was a tough sell for our family of four kids but not for the dogs. They were in canine heaven. Our new home backed up to a beautiful lake, a protected wildlife preserve where there lived a variety of birds, among them geese, herons, swans, and hawks. A farmer's field lay on the other side of a stout hill, and woods rimmed the area beyond that. We'd relocated into doggy dreamland, and the open field was their romper room.

Barely a month into our new home, my husband and the kids were out front with the dogs, throwing a Frisbee. The remnants of a late evening sun hung in the strawberry-tinged sky as I cleared dishes in the kitchen, windows thrown open, enjoying the echoes of laughter from the kids at play. Their sudden screams pierced the air.

I ran to the door. The two youngest met me, incoherent with tears and shock. At first I couldn't comprehend their unfinished sentences. Gizmo did what? He went where? When the truth finally hit, I was as inarticulate as they were. A coyote had taken Gizmo.

We stumbled outside.

My husband and the two elder kids had gone after them. Their yells, disembodied and panicked, rang across the neighboring farmer's field. We waited in silence—our bodies pressed close, their palms sweating into mine. I had no reassurances to give. What could possibly be said after they'd already witnessed the unspeakable? They were unlikely to ever forget the image of Gizmo trapped in the jaws of a coyote.

The others returned empty-handed.

"What happened?" I asked.

"He saw it across the street and just took off," my husband explained. "Wouldn't listen."

I understood then. It was not Gizmo's way to stand by calmly and let a predator lope across his line of sight. As usual, he'd followed his big-dog heart.

"He ignored me," my husband said as he ran his hand through his hair. "I told him to stay. To come. He didn't hear a word I said."

The kids told how they'd taken off after the coyote. How they could not outrun it. How it had taken our beloved Gizmo out of their sight and into the woods.

I replayed their explanations in my head all night. Although I hadn't witnessed it, the images were there, seared into me as surely as if I had. I could see the coyote seize Gizmo and clamp him in its jaws. I could see my husband and kids run toward them, making it only halfway across the farmer's field before, as they watched in horror, the coyote settled Gizmo deeper into its mouth, turned, and sprinted away, leaving only a flash of fur as it disappeared into the woods.

How do you comfort a family swollen with grief and torn apart by guilt?

In the days that followed, my husband searched for Gizmo. He took our Labrador with him, looking for even the smallest of traces—Gizmo's collar perhaps—and bracing himself for a grisly discovery. He found nothing at all.

My own sorrow couldn't compare to the kids' heartbreak. They hadn't wanted to move, and this incident hardened their hearts against everything unfamiliar to them—their new home, the strange neighborhood, their unwanted new school. They hated everything about the move. Most of all, they hated the empty place in their hearts that had belonged to Gizmo.

"Where you do think he is now, Mom?" my young daughter asked every night.

"In a better place," I replied.

"I hear him barking in the dark, after everyone's in bed."

"I know, honey. It's only a dream."

A storm three nights later damaged some of our landscaping. Mid-afternoon, while talking to my husband on the phone, I walked out the side door, rounded the corner of the garage, and halted. Words crawled up my throat and stuck there. My mouth formed Gizmo's name.

On the other end of the phone, my husband was bewildered. "What?" he asked after a moment, not understanding.

"It's Gizmo," I repeated, but this time unsure.

The white Shih Tzu walking up the driveway was not bounding toward me in his usual exuberant way. Exhausted and bedraggled, he limped with slow, measured steps. When he saw me, he stopped; he could go no further. I dropped the phone and ran to him.

It was indeed Gizmo. He had come home.

The veterinarian was in disbelief. Our tiny dog had managed to find his way home through the woods to a place we'd lived in for barely a month. Examining him, her face folded into grim lines.

Even I could see how badly maimed Gizmo was, how glazed his eyes were.

Gizmo turned to me as the vet probed. An aching emptiness filled the dark eyes that had once lit so expressively. I felt as if he were no longer there.

The vet delivered the verdict: Gizmo had a punctured lung, infected eyes, and a leg injury. What shocked me more was how severely bitten he was. The flesh had been ripped open in multiple places by a large, predator's teeth—more than forty bite marks alone on top of his head.

The coyote had not given up easily. But neither, it appeared, had Gizmo.

His survival was a mystery—and a miracle. Maybe the coyote had loosened its grip and Gizmo had managed to scramble away. Perhaps he'd hidden, squeezed in where the coyote couldn't go, beneath an overturned log or between the brambles of a tiny, hillside cave.

The vet put Gizmo on painkillers and antibiotics.

"He deserves to live," the vet commented. "We'll make sure he does."

The kids were speechless. They wanted to hold him and stroke him, to see for themselves that it was really Gizmo. It took a lot of convincing to keep them from overwhelming him. We let him have the space and time he needed, the comfort of sleeping in a safe place, the routine and normalcy he'd been used to until then.

Gizmo didn't eat for almost a week. He didn't interact nor move beyond his water bowl and his bed. He nipped half-heartedly at anyone who tried to touch him. But gradually, as he began to heal, Gizmo came back.

I can't say he's changed all that much. Gizmo still believes he's a big dog. He now runs with new friends in the farmer's field, all of them eighty-pound or bigger dogs, and he still plays with all the ferocity and fervor of a dog twice his size. But I like to think he has a new respect for unknown animals. Though he no longer chases after coyotes, he does continue to warn them off with bared teeth and a snarl or two. The coyotes always lope away, and Gizmo feels he's done his job. That's good enough for all of us.

—J.J. Morgan

A Boy and His Dog

Each time I went up Grayson's Holler to check on Donnie, a patient of mine with leukemia, the five-year-old would come running to see me. I long suspected he had a crush on me. With his honey-blond hair and fair skin, he blushed every time I spoke to him, and the light-brown freckles scattered across his nose seemed to dance over his tiny face when our eyes met. He liked to walk beside me and fill me in on any unusual happenings up the holler. If he saw something he thought I needed to see, he'd pull me toward that object. At times it was more information than I needed to know.

"Timmy's daddy got stung by a bee on his pee-pee. Ya need to see it? I can take ya there."

"I'll check with Timmy's mama to see if he needs help, okay?"

He shook his head in agreement.

Timmy's dad declined treatment or even discussing the injury.

So it was no surprise when Donnie ran excitedly toward me as I got out of my car one warm summer day. He was dressed in a worn red T-shirt and denim blue jeans that were much too long. Holes in the jeans exposed his scraped, muddy knees. But instead of his usual impish grin, the little fellow had a troubled look on his face.

"Can ya fix my dog for me?" he asked, tears running down his cheeks like rain on a windowpane. "My dog got bited; he's in a bad way. Can ya fix his belly, nurse? He don't look good. I'm afraid he ain't gonna make it. Nurse K, ya gotta help, ya just gotta."

"Donnie, I don't know much about doctoring dogs," I responded.

"Oh, you'll do fine. I done told him you can fix his bited place."

I smiled appreciatively for his confidence in my abilities to repair his pet.

"I have to check you out first and see how that sore on your leg is healing. Then we can look after Tramp."

"But I'd just die if anything happened to Tramp. He's my whole life, my bestest friend in the world, and he sleeps with me and protects me from the bad blood cells. If he isn't with me, I get so cold I can't sleep."

I could see the lad was emotionally troubled and knew I wouldn't have his cooperation if I didn't at least check on his old dog first.

Donnie led me to the injured dog, and I followed with trepidation. The large brown and white animal was lying on his side. Sweat forming on my brow told me I was apprehensive about approaching the injured animal—and rightly so. He lifted his head, peered at me with yellow-green eyes, and growled. It was obvious that the injured creature wasn't happy to see me and most likely would not readily take to my medical assistance.

Donnie sat down beside his dog. "Tramp, this here is Nurse K. Remember? I told ya about her. She helps do all kinds of things for sick people. She makes me feel better, and I know she can help make ya better. Ya gotta let Nurse fix your sore."

If the dog could have verbalized, I was sure he would have said, *Yeah, right—after I munch through both of her trembling hands.*

Paying no mind to my fight-or-flight mechanism, I patted the dog's head and spoke to him in a low, soothing tone, "Tramp, it's going to be okay." Though I was not convinced that I could, indeed, take care of the hostile dog, I went on in a calm voice that belied my racing heart. "Donnie is my helper. Please try to ignore your instinct to gnaw me in half."

My mouth was so dry that my teeth stuck to the insides of my lips. My hands were sweating, but somehow I managed to get on a pair of latex gloves. Donnie donned a similar pair. Donnie was overjoyed to put on the oversized gloves and play doctor to his pet. His tiny fingers were lost in the gloves, and the ends flapped like ducks taking flight.

Examining the dog's skin, I saw several tears in his hide. The most severe one was on his left side, and the fur around it was matted down with dried blood. He had obviously been in a dogfight. Throwing caution aside, I poured peroxide into the wound. It immediately bubbled up and got frothy, like pouring beer into a cold mug.

"Wow! I never saw any bubbles like that come out of a dog before," Donnie exclaimed in his little boy voice. "Is he gonna bubble like that forever?"

"No. The liquid I poured into his sore will clean the germs out. I'll leave the bottle for you, and if it gets all sticky again, just pour a little into the sore."

"See, I told ya! You are doing just fine," he said with confidence.

Then, thinking of how inquisitive Donnie was and in the spirit of safety, I told him, "Don't pour it on anything or anybody else. And don't drink any of it, because it will make you very sick. Okay?"

"I promise I won't. I'll just use it for my Tramp."

"On second thought, let me give it to your mama to keep, and you can let her help you with Tramp."

"Okay. Mama will have to put on them gloves if she's gonna help me, though."

I gave several pairs of gloves for him and the peroxide to his mother. We sat a few more minutes, until I realized I had no sterile water with me to rinse the dog's wound. They had no running water in the house.

"Donnie, get me a cup of creek water."

He moved swiftly and returned with a can full of the clear creek water.

"You go ahead and pour that into where the bubbles are," I instructed him.

After the child had rinsed his pet's wound, I handed him a tube of triple antibiotic ointment, and he spread some onto the dog's damaged skin. I showed him how to apply a dressing to cover the injury. Tramp was not thrilled with the bandage, and within seconds, he'd shredded and removed it with his long white canine fangs. That was enough to convince me that Tramp didn't really need a dressing.

It warmed my heart to see Donnie snuggling with his beloved pet. I knew he didn't feel all that well, yet he still pushed forward, making sure his faithful companion was there by his side. He had the most serene look on his face as he curled up beside the dog and wrapped his small arm around him.

Donnie agreed to let me check his leg wound as long as Tramp was a part of the examination. And I knew the dog was observing every move I made while I treated his young master's wound. The dog recovered, and the boy was forever grateful to me for fixing his dog.

On Donnie's sixth birthday, I gave him a stethoscope. I showed him how to listen to his grandma's heartbeat and the sounds of her intestines busy at work digesting her last meal. He was thrilled and described what he heard.

"Granny's got bubbles in her tummy," he said. "And when I listen to Tramp's chest, his heart goes *bumpty-bump*."

What a wonderful inquisitive mind he had. Donnie was so excited with his stethoscope that he got other kids in the holler to come listen to his granny and Tramp's perfectly healthy heart and intestines.

Her laughter was mingled with tears and I couldn't restrain my laughter when she told me about the last round of children that Donnie had brought home to inspect her. "He'd make a darn good doctor. But we don't have the money for him to go to college. So I reckon I'll just let him listen on me," she said wistfully. "They listen to that old hound dog's innards too."

In time, Tramp forgave me, and both he and his master would happily greet me when I came into the holler. I believe that Tramp was every bit as healing as the medicines we were giving Donnie to treat his leukemia.

—Kay Cavanaugh

Taming the Beast

Sometimes marriage is like a hostage negotiation.
You offer up a pizza in exchange for one prisoner.
You wait patiently for your opportunity. Or sometimes you just storm the bank in full body armor,
guns blazing, the spirit of Al Pacino at your side and
a maniacal grin on your face as you run toward certain annihilation. So it was that, patiently, I waited
for my opportunity.

"Honey," I said sweetly one day, offering up a
muffin, "I think we should get a dog."

"Absolutely not," my husband Damon said.

"*Hmph!*" I snorted and ripped away the box of
muffins, leaving his arm suspended in midair and
one muffin crumb falling gently through space and
coming to rest—*plink!*—at his foot.

The next time I tried a less direct route. I
approached from the back of the bank, as it were,
and crawled through the vents.

"Awww," I said, "look at that cuuute puppy! What a cutie! How adorable is—"

"We're not getting a dog," He said.

"*Hmph!*"

Next time, I tried reason.

"Honey," I said, "you know if we had a dog we wouldn't have to worry so much about crime; you know dogs are excellent deterrents to break-ins. And since I'm home alone so much . . ."

I could see him turning this over in his mind. I must have hit on a weak spot. This was good.

"Well, maybe in a couple of years, but definitely not right now," he said.

Bingo! Sounded like a yes to me!

Three days later, I drove to pick out my dog. I mulled over the research I had done on the subject. Rule number one: never, under any circumstances, unless you are crazy or have a compulsive problem with idiocy, *ever* pick the most dominant dog in the litter. They are just plain trouble. Trou-ble.

When I got there, there were eight Brittany spaniels in a wooden box with a blanket and toys. Eight four-week-old bundles of little, fuzzy-brown personality, all of them adorable. One, in particular, stood out. He was twice as big as the other dogs. He was chewing on his brother's tail. He was using his sister's head as a footstool. Every once in a while, he would take a flying leap and land on the pile of fellow fur balls and then stride around the ring like a gladiator preparing for battle. The other pups had no chance. He was so fat and obnoxious that, every time lunch came their way, he would storm through the crowd, push the others aside, and latch onto a teat like he was the king. I definitely was not going to pick him.

He sure was cute, though. He had a certain comforting heft to him, and he snuggled into my lap so perfectly. He had the most adorable brown eyes. But no. No way. I would get one of the smaller, well-behaved dogs for sure.

I picked them all up and played with them, but I kept eyeing The King. There he was, jousting with one of his subjects or sitting on top of another, chewing absently on someone's tail or paw, poking another in the eye, challenging all of them to a romp, and strutting around like he had peacock feathers sprouting out of his butt.

"I'll take him," I found myself saying before I knew what was happening, before I even had a chance to think, before I could extricate myself from my bout of insanity and go back to the world of reason and safety. Love is like that—it sneaks up on you and pounces before you have a chance to get away.

Four weeks later, we went back to pick him up. When we waved goodbye to his family and got in the car, ready to start our new life, I was ecstatic.

My ecstacy was short-lived.

"*Aiieeeeee! Aiiiioooooo! Aeeeeeeiiiiiooooooo!*"

Mere seconds after the car started rolling, the puppy started in on a keening wail, a screaming banshee holler that set my teeth on edge.

"Make him stop screaming!" I yelled at my husband over the din of the wailing.

"What?" he asked.

"I SAID, MAKE HIM STOP SCREAMING!" I yelled.

"He's your dog."

"What?" I said.

"I SAID HE'S YOUR DOG!"

"Oh."

"What?" My husband asked.

"I SAID, 'OH!'" I said.

"*Aieeeeeeeeeeoooooo!*" The puppy continued his banshee screams, acting for all the world as if he were a baby harp seal being bludgeoned to death. We had a four-hour car ride ahead of us.

Three hours and forty minutes later, the puppy stopped screaming and went to sleep. He *was* kind of cute when he was sleeping, not at all like the Tasmanian devil with whom we had just spent the last three and a half hours. He curled up in my lap, his little whiskers twitching as he chased some imaginary rabbit. Yep, pretty cute.

"Let's call him 'Tuck'," Damon said.

So Tuck he was.

We spent that weekend picking up poo and extricating the cats from his jaws. When Monday morning approached, I was apprehensive. I would have to leave him in the laundry room while I went to work, so I crossed my fingers and hoped for the best.

When I got home from work I let Tuck out of the laundry room. One glance inside made me shudder: poo was smeared all over the walls and the floor. It looked like an abstract art project run amok. The dog was covered in poo as well. The room reeked, the dog reeked, and I closed the door. I'll make dinner, I decided.

Damon got home from work.

"Hi, dear. Would you be a darling and take care of the poo? Thanks!" I said brightly, banging pots and pans to indicate that I was *so* busy preparing dinner.

Damon stuck his head around the corner and glared at me. "He's your dog."

"Yes, but I'm pretty sure poo is strictly your department."

He gave me a look that said he was not in the mood for humor.

"Right. I'll take care of the poo," I said.

The first few months passed, as a blur of shoes, furniture, rugs, and anything else that came across Tuck's path disappeared in a frenzy of gnashing teeth and feverish puppy desire. He ate my grandmother's antique coffee table. He ate Damon's new glasses. He pulled the wall-to-wall carpet up in one continuous, twenty-foot thread.

He also took the opportunity to sass us at every turn. Sometimes he would get in my face and growl at me, obviously trying to bully me into giving him his way.

"You need to be more dominant," Damon said.

"Screw you."

"That's better," he said.

One day we watched a documentary on the wolf man—a man who actually lives with a wolf pack in an English zoo. The man was clearly off his rocker, but he had managed to become accepted as the alpha male of the wolf pack. Damon was transfixed. He got down on all fours and started growling at Tuck, showing his teeth and acting out a display of dominance á la the wolf man. He channeled his spirit animal—whether it was wolf, lion, or armadillo, I'm not exactly sure. He beat his chest. He peed on the couch, metaphorically speaking. In the back of his trousers, I swear his vestigial tail started to fluff out a little bit. It was a display known to the ages as "I am male, hear me roar."

"Now I've seen everything," I said.

Tuck tilted his head and cocked an ear up, clearly puzzled. *What were these two crazy humans up to now?*

"Now, you try it," Damon said.

"You're nuts," I said.

"Just give it a try. This is how dogs show dominance. We have to show him we are the pack leaders."

"*Hmph!*" I said. But I got down on all fours anyway and gave it a try. "*Grrrrr!*"

Tuck looked at me quizzically.

"Again. This time with more spirit." Damon said.

I looked at him like I wanted to show him where to put his spirit, but I tried again anyway. "*Grrrrrrrrr!*" I growled and showed my teeth.

Tuck seemed to quiet down a little bit. Maybe we were on to something.

A few weeks later, I took Tuck for a hike in the woods. When I stepped into the brush for a pee, he must have missed me and headed back in the other direction. The result was that we lost each other. For the next twenty minutes, I ran back and forth along the trail, frantically calling his name. Until that moment, I hadn't realized how attached to him I'd become. Now I knew—that little bundle of trouble was so dear to me, I didn't know what I would do if I lost him. The realization hit me like a punch in the stomach, and I ran until I could barely breathe, calling out to him and crying.

Finally, I heard a faint bark in response. He had heard me! We ran into each other's arms like a scene from a Meryl Streep movie. He had been as scared as I was, and he slathered me with kisses, nearly knocking me over in his joy. I knew now how much I loved the little guy, despite his weakness for antique furniture, rugs, shoes, and poo.

Little by little, Tuck evolved. One day I noticed that he raised his leg to pee for the first time. "My little boy is becoming a dog!" I exclaimed proudly to no one in particular. I had evolved as well and was now clearly showing signs of having crossed that fine line between dog owner and kook.

Damon was still resistant, however. Mostly he regarded Tuck as an annoyance and as one more thing to have to deal with, like taxes and traffic jams.

It was around the time of Tuck's first birthday that I arrived home one day to find the house oddly quiet.

"Hello?" I called out.

No answer. I wondered where the husband and the dog had got to. But as I mounted the stairs I heard someone talking in the bedroom.

"Who's a good boy? Tuck's a good boy! Who loves Tuck? I do! Who's the best boy? Tuck is!"

I crept around the corner and peered in. There was Damon, wolf tamer, in his underwear and socks, petting the dog, who had all four paws in the air, eyes closed, and legs splayed in an ecstasy of petting and belly rubs. It was a happy scene. Damon had become a convert. I jumped into the middle and snuggled in like Goldilocks and the two bears and exclaimed, "Now our little family is just right."

But then, love is blind. Thank God for that.

—*Elizabeth Brewster*

Sleeping Dogs

"Mom, I've found a poor little stray dog wandering in the road."

Now, I'm an animal lover as much as the next mother, but it was one o'clock in the morning and, not unreasonably, I was ready for bed.

"Don't worry, Kate. I'm sure he'll find his way home okay," I said, yawning and stirring my hot chocolate.

"Well, the thing is, Mom, it was raining really hard and I couldn't resist picking him up. He's in the car."

I stopped yawning. "Oh no, Kate! Not again!"

My nineteen-year-old daughter has a habit of collecting strays. Everything from traumatized mice extracted from the cat's jaws to homeless boyfriends with unsavory kitchen habits.

"Please, Mom, let him stay just tonight, and I'll ring the dog rescue center first thing in the morning."

Kate did that thing where she peers at me from under her spidery lashes and treats me to the full force of her Bambi eyes.

Well, what could I do?

"He'll have to stay outside then; I'm not having him in the house," I said firmly. "And you mustn't wake your father; he went to bed early with one of his headaches."

"Oh, thanks, Mom. That's cool." Kate enveloped me in a soggy hug. Shivering in my wet nightdress, I watched from the front door as Kate dashed out to her car and opened the passenger door. A large, hairy shape instantly leapt out and tore across the drive toward me, barking excitedly.

"Mom, stop him!" yelled Kate.

Well, I did my best, but the dog had other ideas. Knocking me out of the way, he charged into the house and skidded to a muddy halt on my newly cleaned kitchen floor.

"Oh, Mom, look at him! He's soaked," said Kate. "We can't leave him out all night; he'll catch pneumonia and die."

Our visitor was clearly pleased to see me. He stood up with his paws on my shoulders and slobbered all over my face with an enormous putrid tongue.

"You said he was a poor little stray."

"He seemed much smaller in the dark," admitted Kate, grabbing his collar. "I think he might be an Old English sheepdog."

"I don't care how old he is, he'll have to go in the garage," I said. "We can't have stray dogs in the house, particularly big, hairy ones."

Kate sighed. "Perhaps we could give him a little drink first. He's looking at your hot chocolate."

He wasn't only looking, he was drooling copiously.

"He'll have to rough it and make do with water," I said, filling up a bowl and slipping him a biscuit.

"I'm going to call him Harry," said Kate, who'd read everything J.K. Rowling had to offer.

"Don't start getting attached," I warned, watching as Harry sucked and slurped his water, creating a tidal wave across the floor. "Now, out to the garage with him." Kate took hold of his collar and pulled. Harry sat down and pulled in the opposite direction, making pathetic little whimpering noises.

"Mom, he doesn't want to go. It'll be freezing out in the garage. You always taught me to be kind to animals, didn't you?" Kate did her Bambi impression again.

Well what could I do?

I relented slightly. "Okay, well I suppose he could stay in the kitchen. We'll find him an old rag or something to sleep on."

"Oh, thanks, Mom! You're cool."

"Just don't tell your father," I said, heading for the stairs in search of a nice fluffy blanket.

Harry, who seemed keen to help, ran upstairs ahead of me. I made a grab for him and missed. "Kate, quick! He'll wake your father."

Too late.

Harry had bounded into the bedroom where Jim was sleeping.

I peered round the door. Harry had wasted no time. He was stretched out on the bed, next to Jim, head on the pillow, a look of ecstasy on his scruffy face.

Well, what could I do? It was time to take control. "You'll have to get him out of there first thing in the morning," I said firmly. "I'll sleep in the guest room."

Jim was more than a little surprised to wake up next to Harry in the morning.

"Talk about dog breath," he complained, scratching the itchy pink lumps that had spread up his arms during the night. "I thought it was you."

He took it pretty well, considering.

Kate, meanwhile, had found a phone number engraved on Harry's collar. It seemed he wasn't a poor little stray after all.

"Didn't you think to look last night?" I was cold and irritable after a sleepless night on the lumpy mattress in the guest room.

"It's really faint," pouted Kate. "I couldn't read it in the dark."

I had a feeling she hadn't tried very hard.

"Well, this is absolutely the last time I'm taking in any of your flea-ridden animals," I said, pouring warm milk on Harry's Weetabix. "Your poor father's bitten to death, our bed's crawling with wildlife, and just look at the state of the kitchen floor."

I was in the middle of burning our bedding when Harry's mum arrived to fetch him. It turned out his real name was Buster.

"Thanks for looking after him so well," she said as Buster slunk off to hide under the table. "He's always trying to escape; I've no idea why."

"Well, he's obviously used to living in luxury," I said. "He insisted on a nice comfy bedroom."

"Did he really?" Buster's mum raised her eyebrows in surprise. "He's an outdoor dog at home; he lives in a kennel on the farm."

We all turned to look at Buster. His head was thrown back and his tongue hanging out—almost as though he were laughing.

—*Eileen Gilmour*

That Sheppi Smile

"She's at it again," I called to my husband.

Outside our window, Sheppi, our Australian shepherd, walked by, head held high, higher than usual. From her mouth swung a sable puppy, legs wriggling, mouth open and squeaking.

I knocked on the glass pane. Sheppi set the pup down, bowed her head, looked up at me, and opened her top and bottom lips, exposing a full set of teeth. We called it "the Sheppi smile"—that sheepish grin she flashed when she got into trouble, that gleaming smile she used to greet us.

Joining her outside, I reached down for the pup, shaking my head with a slight laugh, "Where were you taking this little guy, you naughty girl?"

She continued to bob her head and smile. I held the newborn close, his eyes still unopened, and watched how his pink tongue curled and his puppy-thick ears twitched. He snuggled into the palms of my hands as Sheppi stood up on her hind legs, her black and white muzzle gently reaching for him.

Sheppi had done it again, taken one of Meg's puppies. I checked Sheppi's whelping box, and sure enough, not only her own four but also the rest of Meg's little collie crosses cuddled together in one snoozing pile of pups.

"Sheppi, you've stolen them all again, haven't you?"

For some reason, she just wouldn't leave Meg's litter alone. Perhaps she sensed how undernourished Meg still was. Only a couple of weeks before, Meg had wobbled into our veterinary clinic on stick-thin legs with a bellyful of pups. A man had handed the end of her tattered rope to my husband, "Doc, I found her lying in my barn. Would you take her?"

Sheppi had watched intently as Glenn examined and treated the stray and as we pampered her with a heated shelter and full bowls of food and water. Soon after Meg whelped, Sheppi peeked in the partially opened stall door and, with her ears standing at alert, listened to the pups squeaking in the hay. At first, Meg stayed close to her litter, but after a couple of days, she left them crying. Before long, Glenn and I started supplement feedings. Sheppi would stand beside us as those hungry mouths slurped heated milk replacer from tiny doll bottles, giving us a serious look that seemed to say, "Meg's just not caring for them like she should."

After Sheppi started taking Meg's pups and tucking them in with her own litter, Meg would scratch on our front door, whimpering. I would gather them up and return them, then try to barricade the stall against our black and white Aussie thief. Nothing worked for long. Soon Meg gave up and let Sheppi nurse and raise them along with her own, and in a few weeks, under Sheppi's care, they grew large and fat.

When they were old enough to wean, both sets of puppies would still dart for Sheppi and latch on to nurse, a scramble of little legs beneath her. As she journeyed by the vet clinic adjoining our home, clients would laugh and point out how she looked like a giant, multilegged caterpillar walking by.

That wasn't the end of our Sheppi's mothering, though. When she started to nurture two Nubian goat kids brought in for treatment, we referred to her as "mother of the year." The newborns, bleating weakly, were barely alive after being delivered on frost-covered ground, their tongues cold, their palates frigid grey. My husband told their owner, "It's doubtful they'll survive, but we'll give them a chance." After injecting them with vitamins and administering intravenous fluids, we blanketed the floppy-eared kids and bedded them down beside the fireplace while we tended to other patients.

Later, when we checked on them, we found Sheppi had slipped into the box, curled around those stiff, icy bodies, and licked them until their heads finally wobbled upright and their tongues were tinged pink. Sheppi continued to tend to both of them as they struggled to stand on their shaky legs, and she would lay still as their baby goat lips nibbled at her nose and ears.

We began to count on Sheppi, our self-appointed assistant, to help us save the lives of many ailing patients. Many times, she extended beyond her own species to coddle kittens or to snuggle up to weakened lambs. She touched many animal lives, and she brought joy to many people who marveled at her extraordinary caring.

One time, a client brought in a Hereford bull calf, a few days old and orphaned, shivering and dripping wet from a rainstorm. He barely blinked as he flattened his body on the examination table. Again, we made a soft bed on the floor beside the fireplace, hoping the warmth would elevate his body temperature. Alone, he had no mother to comfort him, to sniff him with her hot breath or lick his body with her coarse tongue. It wasn't long before Sheppi took over that job, her pink tongue flashing over his red and white coat, revving up his blood flow. She cuddled against him with her warm body until he thawed, stayed by his side until he gained strength and opened those long-lashed eyes. During his recovery, whenever we'd check on our patient, our "mother of the year" would nuzzle the little calf and then rest her chin across his back.

Over the years, our Sheppi helped save many animals. We saw her foster children often, not only in the clinic for routine care but also out on veterinary ranch calls. We'd spot those grown Collie-cross pups lying on the front porches of farmhouses or playing with children in barnyards or on the streets of our small town. The Hereford calf grew into a one-ton bull and became the fine sire of many calves. We watched 4-H children lead the Nubian goats around the show ring at the Napa county fair and carry away blue ribbons, fluttering from their white denim pockets. The kittens grew into cuddly lap cats and treasured pets. Sometimes, hugging our extraordinary caregiver, we'd point out one of her "saves." She would bob her head, lift her lips, and flash us that shining Sheppi smile.

—*Karen Louise Baker*

Old Dog Smell

"There's nothing wrong with a little dog smell," Granny used to say.

She was referring to the less-than-pleasant odor of Waylon, the hound who spent his days in the field running rabbits. He often returned from the hunt dripping wet or caked with dirt and ticks. And boy, did he get smelly. Waylon would then subject everyone to his mustiness by barging into Granny's kitchen on Sunday afternoons. Granny gave him a cookie to get him back out of the house, and he learned quickly that the easiest way to receive a tasty snack was to come inside.

"Here you go, Wayla Boy!" Granny said as she tossed a cookie onto the sidewalk.

He'd trot toward the cookie, and sometimes he ate it; on other occasions, he buried it underground with the rest of his reserves.

But even after he had gone back outside, much of him still lingered.

"Gosh, he stinks," my little sister giggled as she pinched her nose shut. "He needs a bath!"

"Naw," Granny said. "He's just fine. There's nothing wrong with an ole' dog smell."

That's right. Waylon could do no wrong in Granny's eyes. She didn't flinch when he plopped dead frogs, rats, and rabbits onto her porch. She didn't mind his ear-piercing wail. She didn't even mind his outdoor-rolling-in-dead-stuff odor. In fact, she almost seemed to like it. She liked everything about him.

But Granny hadn't always been so fond of Waylon. Initially, he was my grandfather's dog, a gift from my cousin and a surprise at that.

"We don't need anything else hanging around this house wanting food," Granny said. "Dogs are too much work."

It was too late though. Waylon and my grandfather had bonded. They spent afternoons together out in the lot, the big open space behind the farmhouse. My grandfather messed around with his bottle collection and tinkered with old furniture, and Waylon chewed on twigs. Sometimes, they just sat together on the steps of the chicken house, Waylon sniffing the breeze and my grandfather puffing a forbidden cigarette. They had a special relationship;

they understood one another. But Granny did not understand.

A few years later, my grandfather was diagnosed with pancreatic cancer. It had progressed into a relatively late stage before it was detected. My grandfather stayed in the hospital for several weeks recovering from surgery and undergoing radiation therapy. Granny took care of Waylon.

I was standing on the sidewalk the afternoon my grandfather returned from the hospital. My dad, mom, sister, and I were eager to hug him and welcome him home. We had to wait our turn. As my grandfather opened the car door, Waylon placed his front paws on the edge of the car and licked his face with tail-wagging glee. My grandfather weakly wrapped his arms around his hound, lowered his head, and wept. They were so happy to be together again.

It wasn't too much later that my grandfather lost his fight with cancer and Waylon lost his best friend. For several weeks, Waylon hunted for much longer periods than he ever used to. After he ate breakfast, his white-tipped tail would disappear into the wheat field, not to be seen again until the next morning.

I'm not sure if it was ever actually discussed, but Granny knew what she had to do. She fed Waylon every morning, afternoon, and evening. She marked her calendar with his heartworm pill stickers, and she took him to the vet for his checkups. Granny became his primary caretaker and, with time, his new best friend. Waylon gnawed on acorns while Granny pruned her azaleas. He napped in the sun while she hung out her laundry. They took walks together around the lot. They grew old together on the farm.

It's probably a good thing that Waylon outlived Granny. I don't think she could have handled losing him and what their relationship had come to represent. Until her last day, Granny took care of that dog. And he took care of her too. He helped heal her heart.

I will always remember the sound of Granny's voice as she called Waylon to the house for supper. "Wayla! Come here, Wayla boy," she hollered. And a few minutes later, he would come trotting up the steps, dirty from his last hunt. But before she set down his food, she stroked his dusty coat. There is nothing wrong with an old dog smell.

—*Melissa Face*

Buffy, the Pigeon Slayer

Buffy looks like a stuffed animal come to life and she is about as bright. She is the sort of poodle mix that attracts every child on the sidewalk. Most don't even stop to ask permission before hugging her. She was made to be petted.

We adopted her after a neighbor moved away and abandoned her. Our older dog, Dante, bossed her around. He told her where to sit, when to go out-side, when to eat. Dante is a smart dog. He actually says "out" when he wants us to open the door. He obeys commands. Buffy never really needs to be told what to do. Her job is to be a cuddly, friendly pooch, and that's all we expected of her—until the day she killed the pigeon.

She'd lived with us for five years and still couldn't find her toy bunny if we hid it behind our backs. Poodles are supposed to be hunting dogs; not Buffy.

The only thing she hunted was more admirers—and *they* found her.

It was a normal day. We fed the dogs before eating our own breakfast. They played in the back yard while we ate. Then I went upstairs to get ready for work. The door to my bedroom was closed. That was unusual. I opened it and saw a dead pigeon lying in a patch of sunlight on our gold shag rug, surrounded by a perfect ring of feathers. The scene was reminiscent of an Aztec sacrifice. The bird's iridescent throat glittered blue and green. Buffy growled.

Where was my dog? My Buffy who forgives instantly if I step on her or if a child pulls her fur? My Buffy who runs smiling to greet me when I come home? My Buffy who loves me no matter what and is never angry?

My Buffy growled.

Sweet, cuddly, charming Buffy, the dog who loves everyone, dug her fangs into the bird's chest while her paws pried open the bird's ribs. Blood poured onto the rug. Buffy growled again. My lap-snuggling stuffed-animal-come-to-life made guttural sounds like a savage wolf. In an instant, the bird's heart and liver were down her gullet. She licked her lips with more gusto than she ever showed for my homemade chicken soup. Then she looked up and smiled at me. I'd never seen that smile before. This was the smile of accomplishment, of a heroic deed well done.

I found myself watching in admiration. Buffy is a dog, after all. She is genetically descended from a wolf. But Buffy has an innocent, loving face. I never thought her capable of killing. I called my husband to witness her feat of hunting prowess. We'd never had a dog that could catch and kill a pigeon before.

Buffy hadn't feasted outdoors, where she could have suitably impressed the other pigeons with her deadly jaws. Our yard and rooftop are crowded with pigeons, because our next-door neighbor likes to feed them. We do not like to clean up their poop or listen to their greedy warbles. I had an instant wish that Buffy would slaughter all of them. But Buffy had brought the dead bird through the dog door, through the living room, and up the stairs to my bedroom before beginning her feast. She had even closed the door.

Perhaps she thought it was homage to my husband and me. But she either didn't like being admired while she ate or only wanted the best parts. Once the heart and liver were gone, she lost interest in her kill. Briefly, she took a few dainty licks at the blood, then abandoned her quarry and walked out of our bedroom as if the day had become ordinary again.

How do you clean up after an Aztec sacrifice? What did the ancient priests do after they removed the beating heart and fed it to the gods? I'm not much for ritual.

I put a plastic bag over my hands and scooped up the dead bird. It felt shockingly hot as I carried it to the outdoor trash can. I returned to my bedroom, picked up the feathers, and tumbled them into the compost pile. Finally, I scrubbed the blood from the rug. Our cute, fluffy, little Buffy dog was now a priestess. What other changes would take place in our household?

Afterward, I went into the yard and whispered "Buffy" to the gaggle of pigeons awaiting handouts from my neighbor. They scattered in a whoosh of wings and warbles. Not a pigeon remained in our yard.

Dante, our older dog, our smart dog, who had never caught a pigeon in his life, gave Buffy his favorite spot on the couch. My husband, who had openly preferred Dante, now went out of his way to pet Buffy and give her treats. In one surprising act of instinct, she had become top dog in our house.

About a month later, when I was sitting on the toilet, Buffy brought me another pigeon. She flounced into the room and placed the broken-necked pigeon at my feet. My first thought was *yuck!* I was not grateful. Poor Buffy. I didn't want dead birds in the house to become a regular event. I didn't praise her. She picked up the bird and ran a few feet from me, teasing me, then brought it back and dropped it again at my feet. Then she ran the length of the bathroom and made ready to play catch. *Yuck!*

I patted my knee—our signal for "come here, so I can rub your head." She came and let me rub her head, but she looked at me with reproach. I tried to ignore the corpse. "Nice Buffy. Good Buffy. Sweet Buffy. If you want to play catch, bring me your bunny."

After I was done on the toilet, I got another plastic bag and put this perfectly intact bird into the outdoor trash can. Buffy followed me the whole time. After I replaced the lid on the can, she looked at it and then looked back at me with pure disappointment in her eyes. She didn't understand why I was so blasé about her catching another pigeon.

But that night, when I put the toy bunny behind my back, she went behind me and found it.

—*Lois Wickstrom*

Sometimes You Limp

I am not sure how I even did it. I might have stepped wrong on an uneven path while we'd hiked up the rocky foothill trails in the nearby Sandia Mountains the previous day. Or maybe it happened when I had decorated the back side of our tall Christmas tree while balancing precariously on the back of our love seat. Whatever the cause, my foot swelled up like a football, and it hurt like crazy if I tried to step on it. My husband Bob and I knew beyond a doubt that I needed to see the doctor. As soon as the doctor read the X-rays and confirmed our suspicions—yes, it was broken—I began to panic. *Not crutches again!* I silently moaned. We'd learned the hard way, from past experience, that I do not do well on crutches.

Just a year before, I had fractured my other foot and was given crutches. Though I practiced and practiced, doing my best to learn how to use the darned things, I never got the hang of it and fell frequently while attempting to use them. One time I fell down some stairs and pulled a groin muscle. That pain was even worse than the pain from my broken foot, and I became terribly discouraged.

The wild commotion and my hollering as I bumped down the steps woke our twelve-year-old black Lab, Norma, from her nap, and she quickly came to check on me. As I lay sprawled across the stairs, I look up into her concerned brown eyes and couldn't help but smile and hug her soft neck, vowing to try harder to follow her calm, positive approach to life.

Despite her age and having diabetes, failing eyesight, and advanced arthritis, our amazing pet was a real trooper most days. Norma just accepted things as they were and took it easy. I often wished I could absorb some of that laid-back Lab attitude to get me through some of my most frustrating days.

When we explained my painful past experience with crutches to the doctor, he politely tried to muffle his chuckles and mercifully let me skip those awkward contraptions. Instead, I would need to wear an orthotic boot.

The doctor assured us that the boot would hold my fractured bones in place as they healed while also, hopefully, helping me to avoid further injury to the foot.

Although the boot was an improvement over the crutches, it seemed like the lesser of two evils. The boot was clumsy and made me walk with a pronounced limp. I tried to stay positive, reminding myself that the inconvenience would be for only six weeks.

I'd been hobbling around the house with the awkward boot for a couple of days when we noticed that Norma seemed to be limping when she walked from one room to another. It was hard for me to bend down without losing my balance and falling over (thanks to the tall, stiff boot), so Bob checked Norma's foot and leg, hoping to find the source of her new problem. He found no wounds or sharp stickers in her paw, so we decided to just watch our fuzzy kid for a day or two to see whether she got any worse.

What we eventually discovered was amazing! Norma was normally a house dog, and due to the fact that she was in her golden years, she spent a lot of her time taking naps. Norma had a favorite rose-colored, well-worn recliner that she seemed to have no problem getting up into and where we'd find her at various times, just resting under the ceiling fan. When she'd stand patiently by the back door, with her injured foot slightly lifted, which was her way of asking to go out, I'd often go outside with her, just to sit and enjoy the fragrant late-autumn fragrances and mild temperatures. Much to my surprise, it dawned on me that Norma didn't limp outside. I hoped that meant that whatever her problem had been, it was healing. So we continued to just watch her for any changes.

Another week went by, and I continued to hobble from room to room and to struggle up and down the stairs when the need arose. Meanwhile, we were fascinated that Norma limped some days more than others. We also noted that Norma's limping seemed to be more pronounced during the daytime, when she was solely with me and Bob was at work. If Bob was home relaxing in the living room, Norma usually gravitated to her "daddy," where she could lie down next to his chair so he could rub her ears in just the right places. Now and then, while they were all cozy, she'd not-too-subtly beg for a salty potato chip, if he happened to be having a snack. It became apparent to us that if she moved around in the room with Bob there, she did not limp . . . at all.

We began to wonder, did our furry friend have an injury or was she imitating me? We'd known for many years that our pets have sensed when we were ill, injured, or sad, but this unique situation truly amazed us. Norma seemed to be empathizing with my situation so completely that she actually limped just like her "mamma" did!

As we suspected, once the doctor declared my foot to be healed, allowed me to discard the boot, and I was able to walk normally again, Norma's limping also ended. Sharing that incredible experience with our fuzzy kid truly made the bond between Norma and me even stronger.

I found a new awareness and gratitude for how much Bob and I obviously mean to Norma and for how acutely she notices our behavior and feels our emotions. I believe that discovery, along with so many other lessons we've learned from our precious Norma Jean, has helped me to become more sensitive to the impact my actions and words have on humans too. Sometimes we limp, physically or emotionally, but now I'm more aware of how my limping affects the people, and pets, around me. Now, I try to smile more often and to frown less, to find more joy and to focus less on sadness, and to project more optimism and less negativity. I may never be as laid back as our old black Lab, but I have learned how to make life easier for myself and the people around me. Thank you, Norma, for that valuable lesson.

—*Lynne S. Albers*

Nobody Beats the Wiz

Outside our veterinarian's office is a dog-shaped statue. It's a good-sized dog, a Weimaraner or greyhound, and it holds a basket of flowers in its mouth. It's surrounded by a bed of pink and white impatiens.

"Looks like a grave marker," Frank comments every time he sees it.

We call it "Cerberus." (After the three-headed dog with a serpent's tail from Greek mythology.)

Wizard, our Cairn terrier, always had a bone to pick with that statue. He would approach it stealthily, head lowered, carrot-shaped tail stiff and vibrating, menace apparent in every muscle of his twenty-pound body. He would circle it twice, his movements punctuated with intermittent growling, knowing himself to be thoroughly intimidating. Cerberus, of course, never moved.

After he finished stalking the concrete canine, Wizard would strike an imperial pose beside it. The statue always maintained its motionless respect as Wizard lifted his leg high and sprayed a stately stream of pee all over Cerberus' concrete feet. Then Wizard would strut into the building, his dominance over the statue clearly established. He repeated this ritual every time we went to the vet.

Dominance was everything to Wizard. Despite his small stature, he'd always labored under the delusion that he was bigger than a Great Dane, stronger than a rottweiler, and more ferocious than the most cantankerous pit bull, and he proved it every chance he got. In addition to Cerberus, Wizard had successfully menaced Labradors, Dobermans, boxers and, once, an enormous creature that must be the Brobdignagian of the dog world. (It was quite the largest canine I had ever seen. I later learned that it was a mastiff.)

Somehow, these animals always backed off. Frank and I had often speculated on why. After all, Wizard was only as big as a good-sized Easter ham. The average rottie could make a snack of him with little difficulty.

But Wizard had the element of surprise. Rotties, shepherds, pit bulls—they're the kings of the dog world. The respect of their canine subjects is their just due. To be attacked by a small Cairn terrier would be, at the least, startling. And Wizard never bowed down, no matter how big his adversary. Nor did he ever come off as second best, either. The sight of large, powerful dogs running away from our small, scruffy warrior was a common one. Whenever this happened, Frank and I would look at each other and quietly chant the slogan used by a local electronics firm: "Nobody beats the Wiz."

Apparently, nobody but Wizard was allowed to beat Cerberus, either. During one visit, we encountered another dog visiting the statue. It was a big black shepherd mix who outweighed Wizard by ninety pounds or more.

The dog was sniffing Cerberus, and Wizard apparently didn't like it. Perhaps it was a question of territoriality. Perhaps Wizard was feeling feisty that day, looking for a fight. Or perhaps it was the shepherd's attire that set him off: a yellow rain slicker and four yellow booties. It certainly set me off, particularly since the person at the other end of the leash was similarly attired. It is my personal belief that, when you dress to match your dog, then you deserve whatever you get.

Wizard must have agreed with me because, without a single growl of warning, he launched himself at the shepherd. The slicker-clad dog let out a startled yelp, leapt into the air, and bolted down the street, closely pursued by his slicker-clad master.

"Sorry," I yelled after them, then, "Bad dog!" at Wizard, who was already circling Cerberus. He did his usual two laps, then lifted his leg and majestically sprayed the statue. "Bad!" I repeated, more sternly. Wizard looked up at me, wagging his tail. In his mouth was a shiny yellow dog bootie.

Nobody beats the Wiz.

A few weeks after the encounter with the shepherd, we again came to the vet's office. But on this trip Wizard would not menace Cerberus. He could barely lift his head, let alone his leg. This would be his final visit, the one that's the worst fear of anyone who loves an animal. This time when we left the vet's, we would be leaving without Wizard.

Soon after we entered the clinic, the technician ushered us into an examining room they had prepared for us. A soft blanket covered the metal table and two syringes sat on the countertop, one filled with a clear liquid that the vet explained was a sedative. The other contained a pink substance, deceptively bright.

It was over quickly, and soon I stood over his small body, my hand on the chest that housed his small warrior's heart, stilled forever now. This time, it seemed, the Wiz had been beaten.

I bent down to kiss his scruffy head goodbye, and I was crying hard when I stepped outside. Rain splattered down upon my head, and it seemed to me that the world was crying, too, grieving for the friend I had left behind.

This time, I didn't look at Cerberus. This time, Frank didn't comment on his resemblance to a grave marker.

As we passed, though, I caught a glimpse of bright color. I looked closer and saw it, nearly hidden among the flowers at the statue's feet: a single shiny yellow dog bootie.

Nobody, but **nobody,** *beats the Wiz,* Cerberus seemed to say.

I stood looking at the silly thing and felt myself beginning to smile. Then, with the rain washing over me, I lost track of my tears and found myself laughing.

—*Jeanne Bogino*

Dog Most Wanted

Several years ago, my husband and I adopted a Shetland sheepdog puppy, sporting a lion-like mane in mahogany, sable, and white. He had almond-shaped brown eyes, a wedge-shaped head, and tiny ears that stood at attention, a flaw that excluded him from being a show dog. His face wore a watchful, intelligent expression, complete with questioning eyes.

On the ride home from the shelter, we were introduced to his loud, persistent bark and his kinetic energy as he raced, woofing, from one side of the van to the other.

"He's so rowdy," my daughter, Christine, said.

Finally, his youthful energy ran out, and he stopped moving, barked a few more times, and then sprawled into my daughter's lap. As she stroked his furry body, his long tail thumped in appreciation.

"Let's name him 'Rowdy,'" she suggested.

"Good choice," I agreed.

Rowdy soon lived up to his name and proved he was a natural-born herder as he made a game of romping with our children in the backyard. At six months, he had bonded with our family and understood several words. But that's when I noticed he'd developed an unusual trait that was becoming a daily pattern: mischief. Rowdy rummaged about the house and disturbed things. I'd find a throw pillow on the floor each morning, magazines knocked off the coffee table, or a pewter chess piece tossed in the corner.

By the time he'd reached the ripe old age of two, we had established a ritual of walking him twice a day. But, each afternoon, I'd also release him outdoors for a mid-day potty break. Sometimes he'd disappear and roam the neighborhood. After one such outing, I found an old sneaker on the front lawn and couldn't imagine where it had come from, so I placed it in the trash. The next morning, a small stuffed animal decorated our front porch. Had Rowdy developed a penchant for hunting?

"Where'd you get this, Rowdy?" I asked.

He stared at the stuffed animal and gave me his best puzzled smile before he trotted off. At that moment, I decided there was more here than met the eye, that Rowdy's beautiful looks and sunny disposition gave him the guise of an angel, but underneath he was a little devil with a penchant for purloining trophies from unsuspecting neighbors.

As the days and weeks went by, more and more articles appeared, and there was no denying it: gutsy Rowdy was a thief. He managed to deliver all kinds of strange booty—hats, empty flower pots, even a baseball glove. If a neighbor's garage door stayed open, something was guaranteed to be stolen. All I could do was collect these items and wait red-faced for the rightful owners to come knocking.

My husband and I decided to keep the pilfering dog inside, but our little bandit even stole from the family. Each evening after retiring to bed, we'd be woken up to the sounds of Rowdy stalking our house. He'd drag the kid's metal toy cars, building blocks, and key rings across the linoleum floor.

In the morning, Rowdy acted as if he were rewarding us with his borrowed pile of treasures. He'd cock his head, bark, and prance around the assorted goods and beg for appreciation. My husband scolded him for his bad habit. But then he'd forgive him and start petting him, accepting his wet kisses. Neither of us could stay mad at Rowdy for long, not with his loyal temperament and loving attitude.

One afternoon, Rowdy darted back and forth across the rear patio, barking up a storm. My husband ventured out and discovered him herding a lengthy black snake into a corner. Rowdy's charming face exhibited pride at his wiggling catch. Using a broom, my husband set the snake free and advised the dog to refrain from trapping any other living creatures.

Finally, a good deed occurred that changed the status of Rowdy's notorious gangster reputation. One summer afternoon, his alert dark eyes spotted a wallet somewhere and he maneuvered it home between his teeth. I guess his thieving heart was meant to be. He dropped it on the kitchen floor by his water bowl. Shocked, I picked it up to check inside for a driver's license and noticed it still held some cash.

I promptly telephoned the owner. He said he had lost the wallet two days ago in our area while climbing an electric pole to replace a security light for the power company. The wallet must have slipped from his pocket, and he'd searched for it everywhere.

I directed him to our home, and he arrived twenty minutes later. When the door bell chimed, Rowdy made his presence known with his repetitive barking. Once inside, Rowdy was hesitant in warming up to the man. Shelties tend to be very good guard dogs because they don't like strangers and are very suspicious of them.

The gentleman was ecstatic to have his wallet back, and he wanted to reward Rowdy. I suggested that he donate some funds to the local SPCA in Rowdy's name. He agreed, thanked me, and left. But the very next day he dropped off a bag of special dog treats for Rowdy.

Rowdy has been a best friend to our family for years, and like his well-worn blanket, his friendship has hung in there through thick and thin. As Rowdy aged, he slowed down in his mischievousness, but at times he still continues his ritual of stealing objects and bringing them home. Because of his seedy reputation, the neighbors know where to come when they find anything missing.

If the police printed flyers for wayward dogs, I believe that the heading of Rowdy's flyer would read "Dog Most Wanted."

—*Suzanne Baginskie*

Show Time!

When my husband Gord and I retired and moved to a small farm just outside of Markdale, Ontario, I had the opportunity to fulfill a life-long dream. I had always wanted to raise an Old English sheepdog and, if possible, to show him. We now had two acres of fenced land and the time to train a pup, so we decided to take up the challenge.

Finding the right dog was not easy. We wanted a purebred male puppy with a good pedigree, and such a dog could be obtained only from a registered breeder. We visited several kennels and saw many pups, but at our last stop a cute little scamp wiggled his way into our hearts.

Jody, as we named him, was a joy to raise. He house-trained quickly, had a wonderful personality, and grew into a cute miniature of the handsome adult dog he would become. In fact, both of his parents had been breed champions, and we became convinced that Jody might also do well. So we registered "Rollicking Jody of Belle Farms" with the Canadian Kennel Club and stepped boldly into the show ring.

First, we had to be trained, so it was off to obedience class. Together, Jody and I learned the basics—sitting, lying down, and staying on my command—and then we moved on to walking and trotting properly on a leash. It was a fun and great bonding experience for us.

Next, Gord and I needed to learn about grooming and other tricks of the trade. Old English sheepdogs have very wooly coats that must be carefully looked after. We purchased a grooming table, combs, brushes, scissors, and myriad other items, and studied manuals to learn how to use them to make Jody look his best.

When he was just a year old, we entered him in his first dog show. On show day, great preparations had to be made, starting with a hectic bath. Bathing our playful pup was always an adventure, and by the time we'd finished, Gord and I were as wet as Jody. After blowing his coat dry with a hand-held hair dryer, we spent hours trimming and grooming his coat to perfection. The final touches would be applied at the show.

Upon arriving at the event, we set up our equipment and re-groomed Jody, all the while sneaking peeks at the other competitors and listening for his class to be called. Jody was calm and doing well, but Gord and I had not prepared ourselves for the day. We were hot, thirsty, and rather on edge about the whole affair.

Finally, Jody's class was called and we entered the ring. My first task was to "set up" Jody in perfect position and, once there, hope he wouldn't move while the judge was looking over all the dogs in the group. That day, twelve Old English sheepdogs were competing and many had professional trainers. I was very nervous and trying hard not to show it.

When our turn came, a very solemn judge carefully looked Jody over. First, he checked his bone structure and then moved on to his coat and color, paws, teeth and eyes. Next, he had me trot Jody around the ring so he could observe his gait. The judge nodded and moved quickly on to the next dog.

I set Jody in position again and had him looking his best, just in case the judge glanced back our way. The climax comes when the judge has assessed all of the dogs and then dramatically points to the best dog of the show. That day, the judge did not choose Jody, but for his first showing he did quite well and received a third-place ribbon.

After the show, I was fortunate to chat with one of the professional trainers, who was kind enough to offer me some suggestions. The best advice she gave was, "You need to relax, enjoy yourself, and not be so nervous. If you are, it travels right down the lead to your dog and it will show in his behavior. Your dog has a great look and a good personality. You have to help him show it."

About a month later, we were off to participate in another show. This time, I looked after preparing Jody and Gord looked after preparing for our comfort. The weatherman had predicted a hot and humid summer day, so Gord made a great picnic lunch with lots of cold juice for us and a big jug of water for Jody. We were going to have fun! On our way to the show, I told Gord I had a good feeling and felt we would do well. Gord agreed, noting that if I relaxed like the trainer told me and enjoyed the day, all would go well.

We arrived ahead of time, so we decided to enjoy our lunch before the show started. The ice-cold orange juice Gord had packed was especially good, and I had a large glass to help cool me. I had another while we were grooming Jody and preparing to go into the ring.

Because Jody was a junior, our first competition was against both male and female junior Old English sheepdogs. That class was called, and we entered the ring. I tried to stay calm and poised like the trainer had told me, and I really did feel a little more relaxed. It must have worked, because Jody performed beautifully and we received a first-prize ribbon.

Gord congratulated us, and we began to prepare for the next event. The day had grown hotter, and I was ready for more refreshment. Gord was prepared and made sure that Jody and I both had plenty to drink. Jody lapped up his water greedily, and the glasses of cold orange juice I gulped down really hit the spot. Our name was called, and back into the ring we went.

This time, Jody was competing against the senior males and females in the Old English group. I set Jody up and, as before, he stood quietly. I felt very relaxed, and Jody was as still as a statue while the judge examined him. When I was asked to trot Jody around the ring, we loped easily out and back to our place. I felt confident that Jody should be chosen the winner, and the judge agreed. We won first in that class too!

We hurried back to show Gord our new ribbon and to share our excitement with him. There would be a brief rest period, and then the final showing would take place.

Old English are classed as "working dogs." So, too, were other breeds, like the Shetland and the German shepherd. By being declared the Best Old English, Jody had earned the chance to be judged against all of the best of the other working-dog breeds.

By now, the afternoon sun was very hot and the air was stifling, even under our canopy. I poured another bowl of water for Jody, and Gord prepared some more orange juice for me. We worked together putting some last-minute grooming touches on Jody, then off we went to face our greatest challenge.

Jody was now up against the best of the best. Once again, Jody set up perfectly and held his head like a champion. I stood by, confident that the judge was quite impressed with our appearance. When I was asked to take Jody around the ring, it came even more easily than the previous times. I felt as though my feet were barely touching the ground as we moved lightly through our paces, returned to our place, and reset perfectly to wait until all of the dogs had been judged. The judge finished his task, then strode to the center of the ring and turned to face us. I held my breath as he raised his arm, paused, and then pointed directly at Jody and me. We were Best of Show!

Now we could break our pose. I smiled broadly and gave Jody a big hug and loving pat on the head. Gord joined in the celebration, as did others, and after receiving congratulations and good wishes from our competitors, we packed up and headed for home.

During the ride, I was still bubbling with excitement. I praised Jody's wonderful behavior, thanked Gord for all of his help, and marveled at how, after being so nervous at the previous show, I had stayed cool in the beginning and become even calmer as the day wore on. I couldn't believe how relaxed I had been in the ring.

Gord agreed, then chuckled and revealed his secret. "I made sure you wouldn't be nervous today," he said. "I added a little vodka to your orange juice, each time I offered you a drink."

Even though he was driving, I gave Gord a big kiss and Jody another hug. After all, we were Best of Show and I was still feeling pretty relaxed.

—*Betty Hard*

The Dachshund That (Almost) Conquered the World

Truth be told, he was a miniature dachshund, although you could never have convinced him of that. He envisioned himself more of a sporting dog, a retriever perhaps.

Since he came with papers, we felt he should be given a moniker befitting his station in life. We named him "Baron von Muttleheimer." But we called him "Muttley." And sometimes "The Boy" or "Our Boy."

Muttley quickly set up his own daily routine, which generally began with burrowing under the covers of our bed until the house warmed up. There was the necessary trip outdoors, followed by breakfast. Then back outside again, where he quickly became a part of the local congregation of nondescript neighborhood dogs. He especially liked to hang with the solid yellow mixed-breed from next door, apparently regarding having the big guy lift his leg on him several times a day as a sort of gang initiation.

In the evenings, after serving his dinner, we played with Muttley vigorously until he was finally tired enough to go to bed. Then we could retire too. It was obvious who had the upper-hand in our house.

He loved going places and accompanied us pretty much whenever we went somewhere. Besides, we might stop for an ice cream cone, his favorite treat.

Actually, The Boy had taken to car rides quite well. Not content to merely sit on a seat and hang his head out the window like your standard-issue dog, he preferred to position himself on the top of the seat behind the driver, front paw perched on a shoulder to maintain his balance. Occasionally, the paw would migrate down an arm, and he was known to activate the left turn signal when the mood struck him.

No doubt about it: Muttley was a cool dog, destined for greatness . . . at least in his own mind.

When our first daughter was born, he took it in stride, having already established his place in the family. Now, he had additional responsibilities! If the baby cried, he needed to alert one of us to do our duty and take care of this new little person.

About the same time, Muttley started chasing the wild hogs that populated the woods around our semi-rural home. The fact that they outweighed him by about 245 pounds fazed him not in the least. Naturally, my husband and I were interested in saving our Boy from himself, so we made sure the gate on our fence was always secured.

Despite our precautions, it became a pattern that we would hear the *bang-bang* of the gate slamming shut, followed by wild barking and the sight of a red streak hot on the tail of a huge porker or two. How was he getting out? The only logical conclusion pointed to the four-year-old next door, who had shown us his mischievous side on several previous occasions. I had steeled myself to have a conversation with his parents when, one day, I happened to look out the door to see Muttley relentlessly jumping up at the gate trying to nose the hook closure out of its loop. As I watched in utter amazement, the gate swung open and off he went!

This would not be the last time he demonstrated that being about eight inches tall was no deterrent from accomplishing what he set out to do. Interestingly enough, his next caper was hog-related also. It started when I left pork chops out to thaw on the kitchen counter while we ran some errands. Returning a few hours later, we found the chops mysteriously gone. What could have happened? Nothing else was amiss: could there be a pork predator on the loose? The mystery was finally solved when we looked under the dining room table and saw our Muttley looking not unlike a large snake that has just ingested a water buffalo. Nearby lay the remnants of our dinner on top of some butcher paper with obvious teeth marks around the edges. Looking back at us unapologetically, he merely belched.

But Muttley had his gracious side too. Wrapped Christmas gifts were left strictly alone until Christmas morning. It was only when his gifts (and, of course, he always had gifts) were placed in front of him and he was given the "go ahead" that he felt free to demolish the packaging to get to his treasures.

When my husband, an Air Force sergeant, was sent to Korea for a year, Muttley knew his place was with me and the baby girl he felt was his to protect. Settling in at my mother's house in Ohio, he was quick to come to an understanding with her cocker-spitz. It probably helped that Muffy was both elderly and spayed.

The Boy never quite reached the same arrangement with my sister's and brother's dogs, both males. It is an often disputed argument within the family over what actually happened when I was visiting my brother and sister-in-law's home. Somehow, both Muttley and their Boston bulldog, Studebaker Hawk, got out, and while Studie came back pretty quickly, Muttley was nowhere to be seen. Frantic and fearing the worst, we hopped in my car and started cruising the nearby streets. Eventually, we spotted him sitting on a traffic island all alone on arguably one of the busiest streets in Columbus, Ohio. I suspect that Studie, feeling no cousinly love for the small red menace, led him out to that spot and told him this was where all the action was.

Conversely, I have no clue whatsoever as to what caused Muttley, Studie, Muffy, and my sister's dog, Windy, to all get into a free-for-all under the table where their humans were trying to have Thanksgiving dinner. There were no actual injuries, and on the bright side, none of us had had any idea we could vacate our chairs so quickly. The Boy simply found himself a comfortable spot on the rug and lay down. Had he been a smoker, there would have been a pipe in his mouth.

Also that year, Muttley the Fearless faced a new challenge. My mother's house was located on a busy highway. This meant nothing to Muttley, who took every opportunity he could to dart out the front door whenever it opened. On one particular occasion, I wasn't even aware he was out until I heard a cacophony of screeching brakes. Soon a neighbor came to the door with the awful news that a small, red dachshund had been hit by a car. Could it possibly have been my dog?

Heart in throat, I ran toward a small crowd of people who were gathered around a pitiful object on the sidewalk. Wanting to be protective but fearing being bitten by a frightened, injured animal, they were relieved to see me. I picked up the dazed-looking dog and ran back into the house. Gently placing him on the floor, I dialed the vet's office—and was greeted by a receptionist who could not have been more indifferent to my frantic pleas for help. She put me on hold. While listening to the pleasant music on the line, I plaintively called out Muttley's name, as in, "Are you all right, Boy? Speak to me!"—or words to that effect.

Eons passed, and still I held on, watching the pitiful but amazingly intact little creature at my feet. Then slowly, gradually, a miraculous thing happened: That small but mighty dog first lifted his head and looked around. Then he stretched and got to his feet (all four of them). A hind foot came forward to scratch behind his ear, and off he ambled, presumably tired of the drama, headed for his food bowl in the kitchen.

Gently, I replaced the phone receiver on its cradle.

Eventually, my husband returned from Korea and we moved on: man, woman, child, and dachshund. Muttley made himself at home wherever we went.

Although certainly not your groveling type around humans, he nonetheless held no particular grudge against anyone of that species. He didn't blame my mother-in-law when she tripped over him and broke a few of her ribs. She freely admitted it was her fault for being in the way.

He only ever bit someone once, and even that was a miscalculation. The whole thing centered around a little boy getting too close to him while walking his dog past our patio. Muttley saw it as an invasion of personal space, and soon it was hard to tell dog from boy from dog. Neither dog emerged from the resulting fracas with so much as a scratch, but, unfortunately, the child had a small bite on his hand. Only a self-report to the authorities along with his up-to-date vaccinations saved him from being incarcerated. He would not have done well there. The little boy was fine. But we still felt bad.

We were still recovering from that when we took a day trip to the shore. Making the most of a truly beautiful day, we were strolling along the pier with a leashed Muttley prancing along in front of us. Apparently, the lead was a bit too long, because Muttley decided the thing to do was to sniff a lady who had the misfortune of being squatted down at the edge of the boardwalk peering at something in the water. To say we retreated quickly would be a gross understatement.

Undaunted, Muttley continued on to his next adventure. But this turned out to be the closest he ever came to annihilation. We had been living in north Texas for a few months while my husband went through a technical school and were now packing up to move. During our entire stay in Texas, Muttley had taken exception to the looks of the dog down the street. On every walk past the yard where the miscreant dwelt, I could count on malevolent stares, growls, and baring of teeth on the part of both dogs. Somehow, the day of our departure, Muttley must have known it was now or never. It seemed to bother him not at all that the dog was big nor that his name was Satan. Muttley was apparently working on the David-versus-Goliath theory. Satan had managed to find a way out of his fenced fortress just as we were passing by. We shouldn't have been surprised by this time, but when we got the dogs separated, there was no blood on Our Boy. However, he did keep a low profile all the way to our next base in California.

It was inevitable that one day his frequent, unauthorized darts out the door (any door, anywhere) would lead to the end of our time with Muttley. But it made me sad, anyway. My husband broke it to me that Our Boy had disappeared while I was in the hospital recovering from the cesarean birth of our second daughter. Despite extensive searching, Muttley was nowhere to be found.

I'm glad the new baby took so much of our time and attention; it made things a little bit easier. Still, I worried about Muttley and wondered what had happened to him. Had he been dog-napped, hit by a car? Was he running wild?

It was several months later when I was out and about that I spotted an unusual sight in the traffic. A balding, middle-aged man driving a sporty convertible was stopped at a light. Along the back of his seat was sprawled a small red dachshund, its paw draped casually on the man's shoulder. The light changed, and then they were gone.

Could that have been our Muttley? It would certainly make sense. Perhaps he had tilted at all the windmills our life had to offer him and now it was time for some new experiences. Maybe he was his own dog, not to be truly owned by anyone.

I hope the man in the convertible appreciates his canine pal. And yes, I also hope that the dog I saw with him was my Muttley, not gone from this world, just on the cusp of a new adventure. Maybe he had become the legendary Baron von Muttleheimer at last.

—*Susan H. Miller*

What's Good for Lily Is Good for Me

About a year and a half ago, I did something I'd vowed I'd never do—I bought a pure-bred dog online from a breeder who lived about two thousand miles from me. I used PayPal to secure the deal. The breeder popped Lily into a crate, loaded her on a plane, and sent her to me via American Airlines. This is no pound dog. Lily is an Old English sheepdog with a white face, white ears, and a distinguished AKC lineage. Her official name is "Panda Lily," and it is largely because of her that I moved out of the Hartford suburbs to a farm in Vermont, where the pace of life works better for her and for me.

Our life in the suburbs consisted of a fairy rigid routine based around Lily's bladder. We started the day with a short morning walk. Lily then spent the next seven hours in her crate waiting for me to return from work, when I would release her into the back yard, where she could pee and frolic while I did chores. After dinner, we'd make time to follow the dog-training video that came with her AKC papers to make sure that she obeyed our commands. We'd then take another walk or I would send her around the block with one of my children. While Lily never lacked for love and attention, she grew up in a fast-paced world determined by hectic human schedules.

Enter Lily's life: Sammy and Dutch, two full-grown, one-hundred-twenty-pound male sheepdogs. Enter my life: Bernie, a one-hundred-seventy-pound Vermonter who lives on eighty acres close to the Canadian border. Lily and I suddenly found ourselves traveling north on weekends to visit these three guys. For Lily, these visits set her doggy spirit free. She cavorted outside at will, never had to ask for permission to pee, and clearly thrived in a world where dogs and humans co-existed without pre-planned exercise schedules and container crates. For me, I discovered a world that valued independence and solitude and allowed me to set my own pace.

The decision to move to Vermont permanently did not happen overnight. Those first weekend visits to Vermont planted the seed of possibilities for me, Lily, and my children. It took only a few visits from Sammy, Dutch, and Bernie to make me realize that the outskirts of Hartford, Connecticut, was no life for them. Although Bernie was willing to make the move south, I simply could not imagine how we'd all do it. We planned out a backyard pen and thought about buying a new mega-SUV that could cart us all around, but these plans never survived a three-day weekend in the serene beauty of Vermont. I didn't need to hire a doggy psychologist or a children's therapist to know that what was good for Lily was probably good for me and for my children.

We moved to Vermont, and Mother Nature took over. Instead of looking to me for her every need, Lily now knows what to do—she follows those doggy instincts that the suburbs tried to stifle. She heads out with Sammy and Dutch each morning for a long morning tromp, where they can swim if they want to, roll in dewy grass, or collect cockle burrs in their fur. She stands guard, runs with the kids, or simply sleeps under the porch during the noon-day heat. Lily is living life on her terms.

The same is true for me. I have a less demanding, and yet just as rewarding, job at the local grade school, where I set the pace of my life. I have reconnected with those things that are most important to me. I now spend most of my free time gardening, skiing, and walking with our three sheepdogs, who enjoy my company but don't need me to tell them when to pee.

Now that we all have settled into the rhythm of a rural life, a new and wonderful project sits on our horizon. Lily is pregnant and will give birth to a litter of furry pups in the early spring. I have heard the lectures about how foolish it is to bring more dogs into this world, especially ones that cost money, but what these pundits don't know is that Lily's puppies will mark my own new journey into animal husbandry, a journey with which Bernie is already familiar and one that I want my children to share. As my daughter and I watched Sammy and Lily's courtship this week, I knew that we were in for an experience only found when nature has her way and humans take time to watch and learn.

Bernie is, of course, thrilled that we have moved north to live with him in Vermont, because he can't wait to share all of Vermont's wonders. He can already see how this new setting has allowed me to finally find those things in myself that have for so long been sitting idle. It has also allowed me to let go of the person I've unsuccessfully tried to be for too long. While the suburbs offered me good employment, a busy social life, and excellent shopping opportunities, it kept me too busy to listen to myself. Even my suburban therapist couldn't help me hear the inner voice that was silenced by to-do lists and a frantic pace.

So, while I plan my garden and get ready for Lily's first litter, the dogs chew on the many deer bones that dot the front yard, bones they have dragged out of the woods from last year's winter kill. The sight of these bones spread out over the lawn once would have disgusted me, but gives few Vermonters pause. They understand that dogs will be dogs and that the meat is better off in a dog's belly than in a coyote's. The sight of these bones reminds me how far Lily and I have come. The daily responsibilities here in Vermont are no different than before, but now I do them at my own pace and can carve out more time for me. Lily and I have come into our own. I can't wait to see how motherhood transforms her and all of us.

—Darcy Purinton

No Bones about It

Somewhere it's said that if we give dogs space, time, and love we can spare, in return dogs will give us their all. It's the best deal humans ever made.

Corky Sue Campbell is my handsome and charming silver and black treasure. Forget the "Sue" part, for his middle name is uttered only when he's in rare trouble. He merely asks that I talk to him often, teach him to work, allow him to sit close, and love him unconditionally. If you look into a dog's eyes and see nothing but an icy stare, you're probably not a dog fancier, but when you look into Corky's eyes and see his very soul, your heart will melt.

Corky is the second precious keeshond to come into our lives when we needed him most. My husband was critically ill, so Cork spent months seated close to the wheelchair while gnarly old fingers stroked the pup's head. They both looked forward to afternoons spent on our deck, while Pops spoke of bones and truck rides, though Cork longed for him to toss his ball. Then one day my beloved was gone, so peacefully, so silently, shattering our lives.

Family came in droves to scatter Pop's ashes upon our mountain. Our pastor led us in prayer, I read my special poem, and then we all journeyed to the blossom-covered summit to say goodbye—all except our dog.

Corky brooded against his master's pillow for days, not eating or drinking, as I spurred him on, comforting his grief despite my own. Sharing our sorrow was healing, and my colloquy finally raised us both out of desolate depression.

Toeing up a chunk of early snow while trekking out to feed the stock, I spoke aloud about caring for our ranch with my crippled old body. Rheumatoid arthritis and the loss of an arm left me listing as Corky, Dutch barge dog that he is, pathed our way to morning chores. Would I remember all Pops had taught me about proper care of the animals and equipment? Bent on lifting my burden with his wide smile and love-light shining, Corky slurped cold tears as I knelt to open a bale of hay while virgin snowflakes swirled wildly outside the hay room,

"I need to sound cheerful, huh, Cork? This pity stuff has gotta go, so I'll make a list and get organized.

We're the head honchos now, and I promise not to cry until I'm in the shower, for I know how it upsets you."

And so Cork and I began our first trying year together without Pops. Soon, March roared in, with chinooks and Old Sol goading up patches of green in between snowstorms. Contentment finally embraced us, and I felt like whistling, even with another boot-full of snow . . . until the thefts began. Seven ducks had mysteriously disappeared. Coyotes had wandered near Duck Soup Waterfowl Refuge, but upon confronting Mother Goose's impressive wing span, they hastily retreated. Cork habitually bushwhacked the egg-sucking fox, but now my pup was forced to take up serious sentry duty. Shortly, in the midst of a wild blizzard, there appeared a neighbor dog sloshing through the pond, threatening the flock. Although half the thief's size, Corky plunged into the half-frozen water to defend the fowl. With the mystery solved and neighborly measures taken, there was nary another caper.

After a final May snow, spring emerged with sheets of rain, lightening, and ear-splitting thunder bumpers, driving Cork crazy. While Mother Nature put on her show, he dogged my every step as I locked up at night. Making rounds with cheery chatter and song calmed him and the kitties as they clung close on our big bed, shuddering at old Thor's crashes and rumbles in the twilight. Let a bear wander through these parts, Cork is all macho and full of heroics, keeping us safe and sound. Let there be even one little boom on high, he melts into a puddle of terror.

Torrents of rain finally gave the roof a rest and we relaxed, indulging in our nightly chin-chopper and tummy time. But as I watched the TV news between my toes, we began to jiggle and shake. Terrorized kitties darted away as I held Cork close, quieting his fears. "It's okay, kid, just a little earthquake. I've got you—we'll be fine." Yet, both our hearts pounded like trip hammers.

Summer has arrived at last, and Corky prances and wags at dawn's pink glow, licking my knurly old toes peeking from under the covers, wiggling and woofing as if to say, "Come on, Mom, it's time to get moving." His grin sets the tone of our days, and I jump into my sweats and ponder plans. He can tell by my shoes, or lack thereof, if it's going to be a stay-at-home day, a work day on the ranch, or a day in town. He patiently watches while I put on my face, waiting for the best phrase in his burgeoning glossary: "Wanna go in the truck, Cork?" He whines and rushes for the laundry room to remind me we must feed that bunch of fraidy cats that pop in and out the doggy door. His worst word, of course, "Stay."

"Corky, did you remember the donkey's breakfast? Let 'em out, Cork," I say.

He unlatches their gate into our lush, green acres, where their graze keeps this place in fine fettle. At night, he herds them home, skilled as any herder, even though he hasn't yet mastered closing the latch.

Our weekly days in town are the best, starting with a treat at the bank window and a pat on the head from the grocer's box boy . . . but not before I ask, "Cork, did you go potty?" He rushes from tree to tree in search of the one that conjures up his best pee. "Good boy!" I say, and he knows his favorite seat in the truck is his.

Of course, there are long days when he must stay home to take care of business. Although not keen on babysitting, he knows my promise "be back soon" and has never followed our truck off this place.

Daily duty of the sweet, senior, resident mouser seems to be Cork's bummer job. Our ancient yellow cat lost one eye, is nearly blind in the other, and balks at the new doggy door with its curious flip-flop. "Here he comes, Cork," I say as I gently shove the old guy out onto the deck. "You watch him for awhile, okay?" As if by second nature, Cork jockeys the cat's skinny old carcass away from deck's edge and sure disaster.

And so our first uncertain year as the sole keepers of the ranch has ended on a good note. Family and neighbors were here when needed, but my faithful best pal has quieted my fears, comforted my soul, and saved some ranch bacon more than once. There's no bones about it: My body language and tone tell my dog when I am in need; conversely, sudden motions or the pitch of his bark warn me that it's time to pay attention to him. It's a perfect arrangement.

Our road to mending began in a valley of defeat and despair, but the bond between us helped to heal our sorrows. And that precious keeshond still soothes my heavy heart when a widow's tears sometimes glaze my eyes.

—*Kathe Campbell*

Bulldozer of Love

"Looks like she's beaten the odds," our vet told us.

It was the most wonderful Christmas present we could have gotten. That was a year ago.

This morning, as Cheeni came back from her walk with my husband and our older dog, Mac, she bounded onto the bed where I was writing—all eleven pounds of gorgeous, gray and white furry love.

People stop me on the street when Cheeni and I walk together. "That's the cutest dog I've ever seen," they say. "You are so lucky!"

You have no idea, I think. *You simply have no idea.*

"Check the rescue places first," my husband said when I mentioned that I wanted to get another dog. I could feel Mac getting older, hairier, and more tired as we sat on the big green chair together, watching the evening news.

No parking space was available in front of the animal rescue shelter the next day. I drove around the block, but still found no place to park. Finally, on the third trip around the block, a car pulled out. *It's a sign*, I thought, as I whipped into the spot and hastened inside as if on a mission.

And there she was, in the first cage, wiggling with excitement! I stuck my finger into the cage, and she licked it with her lizardy tongue, rough but gentle, like my grandmother's washcloth. Her stiff hair splayed in every direction. The sign on her cage read, "Fuzz-Muffin."

I went straight to the desk, where four women efficiently ignored me while they answered phones and jabbed at computer keyboards. The place, I noticed, was a mess. I have to get Fuzz-Muffin out of here, I thought. I wonder if I can take her home with me right now.

The woman in charge finally noticed me. "Just fill in these papers," she instructed. "You're the first applicant."

"How soon will we get her?" I asked.

"Well, she needs to get her shots and we need to review the applications. We'll let you know if you are chosen."

My heart sank. "Chosen?" I stayed with Fuzz-Muffin until lunchtime, then called my husband.

"I found a dog," I told him.

"Great."

His response could have been interpreted a number of different ways. I chose to take it positively.

When my husband got home from work we went by the rescue center again. Fuzz-Muffin licked my hand.

"She knows me," I said.

"Hmmm . . ." my husband mumbled. "She doesn't have a tail."

I hadn't noticed that, but did now. Her rear-view was square, like an ox, with only a tiny stub sticking up. It gave me the shivers, like an amputated leg, and I tried not to look. Her fur was matted around the stub, and her whole back moved when she tried to wag.

"She seems okay," my husband said.

I thought he meant her tail, but he was talking about the application—that it was okay to adopt her. As someone who works in the juvenile system, my husband knows that it is not at all hard to find someone to take care of. He knew that a half starved, deformed, lop-tailed dog was easier to find a home for than a sixteen-year-old kid with a rap sheet.

When I went in to see Fuzz-Muffin the next day, she was gone.

"Where's Fuzz-Muffin?" I asked when I finally got the attention of one of the ladies at the desk. I now thought of them as social workers. "How is my application coming along?"

"I'll check the computer."

I looked around. None of the other dogs I saw were cute like Fuzz-Muffin. One of the dogs had only three legs. *These are the sixteen-year-olds with rap sheets*, I realized.

"We don't seem to have your application," the social worker reported, staring at the computer screen.

"But mine was the first one! She took my application," I said pointing to a woman in coveralls cleaning something up off the floor. The woman remembered me.

"Fill out another one," the woman said, her eyes still on the computer screen.

I did. "Judge" I wrote where it asked for my husband's profession; "lawyer" I wrote for me. Under family, I wrote "seven kids—five adopted, four disabled, all grown." I also wrote "refugee camp experience." I wanted them to believe I could handle a puppy.

My husband phoned every day. "When will we know about our application?" he asked, if someone answered.

"She'll be back in the shelter on Saturday," the woman told him. "The foster parent is going on vacation."

Good, I thought. I didn't like this mythical foster parent. She might be trying to alienate the affections of my puppy.

On Saturday, Fuzz-Muffin was back in the shelter, as promised, and she licked my fingers when I put them into the cage. She hasn't forgotten me! It had been ten days since I had applied to adopt her. We checked on our application, just to be sure. Sure enough, they had lost it again! I was beside myself.

As we filled out a third application, the woman was extremely apologetic.

"Sometimes it gets a little overwhelming," she said. "There are so many dogs no one wants. Oh, and we are treating Fuzz-Muffin for giardia," she added. "So she hasn't had her shots yet. We've had a lot of applications for her, though."

"How many?" I asked with trepidation.

"More than fifty."

Was she trying to tell us we would not get her? "But we were the first one," I said. My voice must've sounded desperate. "Our application has been lost twice."

"Here," my husband said, handing the social worker our third application. "When will we hear?"

"Soon," the woman told us. She smiled. I had the feeling she hadn't really thought about it before.

"Do you want to meet our other dog?" my husband asked. "We could bring him in."

The mention of a dog seemed to be more interesting to them than either us or our paperwork, and Mac came in wagging. He sealed the deal with his social worker interview. They petted him and gave him treats. They smiled as they sent us on our way.

We had not been home an hour when the phone rang. It was one of the social workers. "Congratulations! You've won the lottery!" the woman told us. "Fuzz-Muffin is joining your family."

Fuzz-Muffin would need to stay a little longer to finish her giardia treatments and to get her shots, though.

But the next day Fuzz-Muffin was gone again. "Back with the foster family," the social worker said. "She is running a fever." That was Sunday.

On Monday, the social workers were concerned.

"She is pretty sick," they told me. "She has a fever and she is not eating."

Fuzz-Muffin was back, isolated in the back of the shelter behind some racks of dog food and old towels. She looked terrible. I sat on the concrete floor and held her in my lap for three hours. She licked a little pureed chicken and rice off my finger, but mostly she just slept. She seemed completely different.

By Wednesday, Fuzz-Muffin was clearly desperately ill. I took her to the vet across the street from the shelter, who X-rayed her and gave her blood tests.

"She's really sick," the vet told me, but I already knew that. "It could be distemper," she said in an off-hand manner. "She should be put down." She did not look at me when she said it and charged me $500.

"Do you put down dogs when they have distemper?" I asked the rescue social-worker lady.

"We don't, but she may die anyway. I think the odds are about fifty-fifty," she said. "I'm sorry," she added.

I carried Fuzz-Muffin, wrapped in an old towel, to her cage behind the dog food racks. She weighed hardly anything, only 4½ pounds on the vet's scale. She was shaking, so they ran an IV into her neck. She finally stopped shaking and went to sleep.

"Should we bring her home?" I asked my husband that night.

"Distemper?" he asked, to be sure he had heard correctly.

"Maybe the neighbors can take Mac for a while?"
I said and picked up the phone.

It was decided: our loyal old dog would move
next door with the neighbors until we were absolutely sure he could not catch whatever Fuzz-Muffin
had . . . or until she died. We would fence off a sec-
tion of the living room for Fuzz-Muffin to live in.
Someone from the rescue group would come twice a
day to give her a new IV.

On Thursday, we brought her home—for better
or for worse.

Our own vet did a distemper antibody test and
Fuzz-Muffin tested positive. It would be six weeks, he
told us, before we would have a good feel for whether
she would survive.

In the next few days, Fuzz-Muffin went blind.
Over the following weeks, she had seizures, during
which, if not prevented, she would hammer her nose
into the ground until it bled. She lost weight to the
point that I could hear the clunk of her bones on the
floor when she sat. Her eyes and nose ran with ooze,
which I wiped off with the baby wipes I had for my
grandson. Her temperature soared. She chewed, as if
chewing gum, almost constantly. Her hair was stiff
with her own stickiness.

I loved her, though. I held her on my lap all day,
every day, in front of the fire. I never left her side for

fear she might have a seizure. If her life was to be short, I was determined it would be as nice as it could be. She did her business on the deck, and we cleaned it up for her. Our living room looked, as one friend put it, "like a refugee camp." IV bags hung from the curtain rods. Droppers and wipers and bottles of pills littered the antique end tables.

Fuzz-Muffin's distemper titer eventually cleared, but she was still blind and having seizures. With Mac's shots updated, our vet determined it was safe to bring him home again. Mac showed very little curiosity, however, about his new sister. If she got near him, he slunk away. He seemed to know she was dangerously sick.

Fuzz-Muffin, for her part, continued to mostly sleep on my lap. We couldn't tell if she could see yet. But she was eating just a little and had gained a few ounces.

After a few weeks, the vet said it was safe to take her outside for a walk. We put on her pink harness and attached her purple leash. I carried her to the sidewalk, where she cowered in panic and refused to move.

"Not ready yet," said my husband.

About the time her distemper titer cleared, we decided to rename her. Her new name is "Cheeni," which means "sugar" in Hindi. We hoped it would bring her good luck.

Naming a dog is a hard decision. The name has to fit. Sometimes, when Cheeni hallucinated and ran in circles, hammering her nose into the floor, or when she dragged her hind quarters, seemingly paralyzed, across the floor, we called her "Princess Pupule." Pupule (poo-poo-lay) means "crazy" in Hawaiian. Ultimately, her full name became "Cheeni Princess Pupule Fuzz Muffin—The Bulldozer of Love." We call her Cheeni for short.

As November gave way to December, Cheeni seemed better. She could take walks around the block if I picked her up and hid her in my coat when a scary car went by. Mac stopped jumping off the chair when she jumped up. Cheeni gained more weight, and she no longer had to have IV rehydration. She had gone from the cute puppy that fifty people wanted to adopt to the limp hopeless piece of fur (more like the sixteen-year-old kid with a rap sheet that no one wants) and back again. Her struggle was her own, though. Her call to us had been strong, and she pushed her way into our lives with all the strength she could muster.

That's what it takes sometimes. It is why we call her "the bulldozer of love."

—*Kristin Seeman*

An Autumn Romance

Rosie was long past her prime, but her looks were never that important to her anyway. She was part German shepherd and other parts no one had quite figured out. She never got on with other dogs; in fact, she had a general dislike for anything with four legs. Those with two legs she wasn't keen on either, except for the people she thought belonged to her.

She had come to us from a rescue center, only because my sister was picking up a cute cuddly dog and the woman in charge told her they couldn't keep Rosie any longer because she was too much trouble. Rosie looked at her with that "I don't care what they do with me look," and Nan just had to take her. Of course, she turned out to be so much trouble that Nan couldn't keep her either. There was no way Rosie could stay in the same house with another dog, never mind Nan's two cats.

A long drive in the middle of winter brought Rosie to our house. We estimated her age at around two or three. If you tried to pat Rosie, she cowered away. If you opened a door, she took off. If you left anything on the kitchen counter, tin cans or food of any kind, you would find them hidden under her blanket in the corner. Her favorite trick was to watch you unpack groceries, and as soon as you took your eyes off them, she would steal anything you hadn't put away; bars of soap and toothpaste were a particular target. On one of her many disappearances, when someone had been too slow in shutting the kitchen door, she came back with a package of rolls between her teeth, trotting up the driveway as proud as could be. We never did work out where they came from. She liked to take off for a few hours but always returned, usually with something that belonged to someone else—a ball of string, an eyeglass case, anything that caught her fancy.

There was something in Rosie's feistiness we could not resist. The world had obviously been unkind to her, but she was never going to back down. She treated life on her terms—full on and with a will of steel. We admired that, and so gradually she settled in and became part of the household. But beware, unannounced callers! She would bare her teeth and growl at anyone who came to the door, protecting her family. When repairmen called, Rosie had to be locked in another room; she hated having someone strange in her house. With family friends, she was okay once she got used to them, though she always maintained a certain aloofness. Many people asked us why we kept her. Though she was never going to belong to anyone, we had become her people. She loved us and had decided it was her job to guard us; she wasn't interested in anybody else. Rosie was not one of those dogs who would go to someone to be patted or wag her tail for a treat; she would never stoop to that.

So, for eighteen years, she patrolled our yard throughout the day, looking for any intruders, or she would lay with her head under the garden gate, watching for danger. She never came when called. If we took off her leash on a walk, she was gone.

Our yard had become impenetrable. Over the years, she had dug under the fence to get out in so many spots that we had buried boards along the whole length of chain link fence that kept her in the backyard. She liked to be outside, even in the depths of winter. She was always more comfortable there; on patrol and looking for any threat to her territory was her chosen profession. No squirrel or blue jay ever lingered long in our yard; Rosie would tolerate no intruders whatsoever.

One lovely autumn day, I was watching her through the kitchen window—her nose under the gate, as usual—when I thought I saw her tail wag. This couldn't be our Rosie; she was wary of everything.

The next day, around the same time, the same thing happened. I wanted to see what made Rosie react this way, so I went to the front window, and there he was: a handsome, gleaming black rottweiler, leading an older man down the street. This was the first time Rosie had ever acknowledged another dog with anything but a growl. I just had to let her meet this beautiful creature.

So the following morning I watched for them, and when I spotted them, I put on Rosie's lead and headed to the park across the road where I had seen them go. The man was letting his dog run free on the track that runs around the park. As we stood watching him, the rottie caught sight of us and bounded up to Rosie. She wagged her tail as he sniffed her gently. I could not believe it! Rosie had a distinct dislike for any other creature, especially dogs.

The old man came over and introduced himself. He suggested that I let Rosie go so the two dogs could play. Rosie was now twenty, and I had never let her off the leash.

"Where's she going to go, an old girl like that?" he urged.

This was true; she was a lot stiffer and slower than she had ever been. So I decided I could risk it. For the first time in her life, I let Rosie run free with Murdoch, her new friend, beside her. It was wonderful to watch them romp around that park together. She looked like a young dog again. When she was exhausted, the man called for his dog, and Rosie, to my surprise, came too, head held high, tail wagging.

Every weekday for a month, I met the man in the park, and we watched while Rosie and Murdoch romped together. I could feel her excitement when she saw me reach for the leash, and I swear her eyes lit up when Murdoch ran up to her. Then that awful Saturday morning came when Rosie just couldn't get up anymore; her back had gone. We took the hardest journey any pet owner ever makes, her last visit to the vet, and said goodbye to the best dog ever.

On Monday, I went to the park alone with a bag of treats for Murdoch. As he rushed toward me in the usual way, he looked around for Rosie. I knelt and caressed his lovely, gleaming black coat. How could I thank him for the wonderful time he had given her? He was her autumn love. It had taken her all those years to find him, and it was over so soon. The old man asked me if I thought running with Murdoch had been too much for her. Perhaps it had, but I know that for Rosie it was worth it.

—Christine Kettle

Fresh Out of Control

I t's no secret: I'm a bit of a control freak. I like to be in charge, I like to keep things in their place, and I like to know what's on the agenda when I make plans with my family and friends. I've been described as bossy, but I like to think I make very good suggestions for how things could be done better. Because my way is clearly the best way.

Newsflash: not everyone wants to hear me tell them how they should drive or dice tomatoes or arrange their bookcases. And apparently, most people don't plan out detailed schedules for casual get-togethers with friends. While I glance at my watch and obsess over the number of minutes that tick by between cocktails and appetizers and silently fume about how long it's taking until dinner's ready, my friends laugh easily and pour themselves another drink without a second thought about when we'll eat.

It comes as no surprise that my husband is always telling me to relax. "How can I relax?" I ask him. "When there's a stack of paper five inches high perched on the corner of the kitchen table, dirty laundry spilling out of the hamper, and a fine coating of dust on the tabletops, how can I relax?" I'm too much of a type-A personality to relax. I grew up believing in being ten minutes early, asking people to keep their feet off the coffee table, and always using a coaster. It goes without saying that any other behavior would result in disaster.

That's right, disaster. So imagine how ballistic the needle on my organization scale went when my husband and I introduced a dog into our house. Dogs shed. They scatter squeaky toys all over the living room. They leave wet paw prints on the floor after coming in from the rain. They have no ability to control the water that streams out of the sides of their mouth as they drink. How can *I* control *that?*

Turns out, I can't. It also turns out that I wasn't the only one trying to figure out how to control things.

My husband and I adopted Moses in late October. A rescue dog from Tennessee, he was a seven-month-old shepherd mix. We were told he's part retriever, and that news excited us. What's not to like about retrievers? They're happy, friendly dogs.

My husband had a black Lab when he was a kid; they got along famously. The shepherd-retriever pairing seemed like a great combination.

Only, it doesn't seem like shepherd is actually the other part of the mix. Moses is a black dog with pointy ears that stick straight up. He's medium-sized with a tail that's very plume-like. A shock of white fur runs up his chest, and small patches of white dot his chin and paws. He likes to nip at our heels as we walk up the stairs ahead of him, and he enjoys herding his fellow canines at the dog park—not to mention my husband and me and anyone else in the house. When people ask us and we tell them what kind of dog Moses is, they nod their heads and wonder if we've ever considered that he might be part border collie.

Have we considered that? Well, yes. We have also been trying to ignore it. Although border collies are my favorite breed, I had been cautious about choosing not to adopt one. Meaning, I had completely and deliberately avoided the breed. Although border collies are energetic and intelligent, they also require lots of stimulation and activity. My husband and I wanted a dog that would be active with us when we wanted it to be and mellow when we needed it to be, which was most of the time. We weren't sold on the neurotic part of the border collie personality that we'd heard so much about—herding crowds during parties and destroying furniture if they aren't properly exercised. I devoted enough of my time to figuring out how to keep the house looking presentable without having to worry about making sure the stuffing wasn't pouring out of the couch cushions. I didn't really need to add a new member to our family who devoted his free time to seeking out opportunities to rip apart the leather sofa.

But after being asked this question a number of times, my husband and I started wondering if maybe Moses was part border collie. From the reading I had done, many of his characteristics fit the breed. And he certainly could be a force to contend with. Despite my own strong type-A tendencies, Moses seemed to be even more concerned about his schedule than I was about mine. His routine was not to be messed with. Don't think about oversleeping and don't think about taking the shortcut around the block. Food must be presented promptly after the morning walk, and much barking will ensue if it is not delivered on time. The door will be scratched if his need to go outside is ignored, and shoes will be chewed if not enough attention is paid to him when he wants it. Correcting this behavior doesn't get us far. The word "no" holds meaning for all of thirty seconds, and instead of settling down quietly on the floor by our feet after these incidents, he'll raid the houseplants for soil, shred the blanket in his crate, or rip the eyes off his favorite stuffed toys.

B.D., or before dog, I had been the one in charge. I could clean and organize all I wanted, and no one got in my way. Meals were eaten in peace and complimented by conversation between my husband and me; there was no obnoxious barking interrupting our stories about our days. If I wanted to vacuum on a whim, I could. No one chased the vacuum or barked at it while it was out of the closet even if it wasn't turned on. And if I wanted to watch TV upstairs while my husband was downstairs on the computer, I could. B.D., Moses hadn't been there to walk up and down the stairs trying to round us up and make one of us give up our spot to join the other in the same room. I wasn't used to having someone—make that, a dog—tell me what to do and where to sit and when to do it. I knew I could be stubborn, but Moses took stubborn to a new level.

I couldn't very well reason with Moses, so I knew we'd have to meet somewhere in the middle. With Moses in our home now, I've realized that I need to scale back on some of my control-freak behavior. The house is not always going to be sparkling clean, there's going to be water on the floor after he drinks from his bowl, and there will be toys spread out over the living room floor, including random eyeballs pulled off the heads of his dog toys. Life is less predictable with Moses around and not as easy to schedule. It's impossible to know when Moses will need to go out or when he'll need a longer walk or a trip to the dog park. Such spontaneity can't be planned, and I've actually come to look forward to it.

For a dog who's so particular, he's also just as playful. Between the barks and not-so-subtle nudges are lots of licks and tail wags. His quirks are unique, but they make me laugh (and shake my head). I never quite know what to expect these days, and instead of driving me nuts, it's forced me to do the one thing my husband is always asking me to do: relax.

—Kate Langenberg

Smart Girl

My dog never went to college. Nor did she go to obedience school. In fact, she has no formal education whatsoever. Her vocabulary is limited. And the only trick she knows is how to stand like a prairie dog when she wants a boney (which, in her doggy dictionary, means "milk bone"). I've been told I have an impressive vocabulary. And on my wall hangs a hard-earned diploma—tangible proof that I am educated. It's a good thing I have that diploma to remind me that I am smart, because my beloved dog regularly puts me to shame. Well into middle age, I am still searching for that which makes me entirely happy. Meanwhile, Annie has it all figured out. She knows what wags her tail and she knows how to get it.

Annie is a black Scottish terrier, an accomplished con artist, and my best friend.

If I leave her even to walk to the mailbox, upon my return mere moments later, she sits beside me studying my face, as if memorizing every detail in case I leave again.

On Saturday mornings she waits for the cows to pass through the meadow behind our back fence. When they appear, I whisper, "Annie, the bad cows want your boneys."

A fleeting look of word recognition on her face, and she's out the doggy door and into the backyard, prepared to defend her precious boneys from the thieving cows. But Annie's no dummy. Even without a diploma, she knows that those larcenous bovine are big enough to clean her clock and swipe every boney. She still tells them off good and proper . . . from behind the safety of the giant mimosa tree inside the chain link fence.

I, on the other hand, have been known to foolishly honk my horn at the occasional big-rig driver who gets too close. I know they could effortlessly convert me to a speed bump if they wanted, yet I blast away, without the protection of a chain link fence or a giant mimosa tree. Annie would never be so reckless.

She's clearly smarter than I am. But her true genius is revealed when she wants to be scratched. She loves to play tug with me and an old knotted sock. She appears at my side, sock-toy in mouth, as if to say, *Let the games begin!* And they do.

At some point, Annie figured out that, though tug is fun, a good fanny scratching is even better. But with her limited vocabulary, she had to figure out a way to communicate her wishes to me. If a signal worked to bring her one favorite thing, then perhaps with a little quick action, the same signal could also bring her other good things. So one day she came to me with eyes eager and tail wagging, sock-toy in her mouth.

Like the well-trained owner I am, I took the bait, not realizing she was playing me for a fool. "Wanna tug, Annie?" I asked.

The instant I reached out my hand to get the sock, she did a one-eighty, spinning halfway around so that instead of my hand landing on the sock, it landed on her rump. Of course, I scratched her. After all, I am very well trained. Encouraged by her success, Annie must've decided the old fake-tug ruse was a maneuver worth keeping, because it became a regular part of her act. Clearly, my dog has no problem with bold-faced lies.

I'm certain that, at first, Annie thought me an easily manipulated dolt. By now she's probably forgotten that this was ever a deceptive ploy in the first place. She now seems to believe that carrying a knotted sock in one's mouth is the universal sign for "Please, dah-ling, won't you scratch my itchy rumpus?"—much the same way that putting one's hand to one's throat is the universal sign for choking. It's times like these when I feel compelled to pick Annie up and carry her into my office, hold her up to my diploma and read aloud so she can see for herself that I really am smarter than she is, at least on paper. Then I scratch her rump some more, followed by a game of tug.

The truth is, Annie is not at all impressed by my diploma, my amazing cache of knowledge, or even my fabulous vocabulary. She may not have a formal education, but when it comes to manipulation, she is way ahead of me.

If only we humans could so easily get what we want. When I think of the lengths we go to get our kids to clean their rooms, our spouses to remember our birthdays, and our bosses to notice our good work . . . it makes me tired enough to lay down by Annie for a long siesta.

I can learn a lot from my dog. With Annie, there is no big decision process. Her needs are simple so she can zero in quickly on the object of her desire. She doesn't require therapy to sort out the issues of the past, probably because she forgives and forgets before I can even apologize. She plays hard—mostly protecting her boneys from conniving cows and defending us from thieving postal workers who come by every afternoon and open our mailbox. And then she rests hard. So she is rarely out of sorts. She never wakes up on the wrong half of my bed, because she takes her half out of the middle.

Annie may have a limited vocabulary, but when she wants something, she never beats about the bush, though she may get a bit creative sometimes. Unlike most of us mere humans, Annie knows what wags her tail, and you'd better believe, she knows how to get it.

—Teresa Ambord

Big as Life

The baby is screaming, and we still have thirty-six miles to go. The car, stuffed with our travel bags, zips along Pennsylvania back roads through the night. My husband, preschooler, and I are tired and headachy. I took the center backseat at the last rest stop, intent on keeping our eight-month-old content for the end of the trip. But nothing—no teething ring, baby food snack pack, or crinkly toy—is enough to quiet his rage. He is done with this day's journey, and he wants out.

He lets out a particularly high-pitched shriek, reminiscent of the cinema of another age, a lovely damsel upon seeing Dracula. He learned this scream last week when a high fever and throat infection knocked him off his little hands and knees for a few days. When ill, his scream had a weak kitten effect that prompted immediate cuddling and soothing. Now, wholly healthy, he emits screeches that incite a sick-in-the-stomach dizziness. I see my husband place a hand over the side of his head.

"Is he making a joyful noise, Mommy?" my pre-schooler Aidan asks, referring to my label for baby Alec's usual bursts of opinion.

"No, I think this time he has the screaming mee-mees," I say.

He ponders this with four-year-old earnestness.

In a brief pause between the mind-blowing bawls, I twist around, concerned for the most sensitive ear-drums of us all. In the cargo area, a three-month-old Great Dane pup rides in the bottom half of a plastic dog crate lined with fleecy blankets. She is sitting up, watchful, her black long ears swaying to the move-ment of the car. She blinks, some question forming.

I smile at her and murmur, "It's okay."

When the baby lets go another whopper, she lies down but keeps her eyes on me.

I wonder what in the world I've gotten us into.

The quest for a new dog began weeks before. Like many quests, it took me, the main player, to new worlds. I encountered tests and enemies, tricksters and shape-shifters. But, with the help of a wise mentor and strong allies, I brought the sought-after treasure home.

We lost our last dog, a Lab mix from the local shelter, to cancer. She was diagnosed on a Friday afternoon, and by the following Friday morning, we were watching a kindly house-call vet put her to sleep. That last week was, in ways, fulfilling; I loved her completely, fed her chicken and mashed potatoes and oatmeal cookies, and we made the decision to put her down only when her suffering made the right choice obvious. But it was also sudden and shocking, and I plummeted to a pure sadness that grabbed and trapped me not only for that last week but for months to come.

I missed Sara and the way she would yawn and wag her tail simultaneously to welcome the morning. I missed her close attention to last bites of food and our nightly ritual of sharing a bowl of cereal. In the middle of the night, sleeping on the couch when my husband traveled for business, I thought I could still feel her and smell her. But I also missed walking outside six or eight times a day and a set of ears that always listened without passing judgment and the solid, knowing presence that welcomed me home after dark.

Eventually, I thought I might be able to separate missing Sara from missing the companionship of a dog. Sara had completed us; she'd joined my husband and me early in our marriage, moved into our first home with us, and was waiting at the door when we'd brought Aidan and later Alec home. So when the time came, I wasn't merely searching for another dog—I was on a mission to locate a new housemate who would not only complement our lifestyle but also complete our family, at least for the next leg of the journey we all would share.

I knew I wanted a dog whose very size would be a comfort to me. Sara's eighty pounds had served as both a barrier to strangers at the door and a cushion for our tired frames. I read up on several giant breeds and started broaching my idea to dog owners, our vet, and our boarding kennel. Finally, I announced it to my husband.

"I want a Great Dane," I said.

"Whoa." He blinked many times. "Wow. Okay. Why is a Dane the right dog for us?"

I ticked off the reasons: Temperament and training potential. Personality and ability to bond with people. Beauty and nobility.

"And the cons?" These I reviewed at length, especially cost and health concerns. But, after many discussions, we realized we were willing to accept them.

I found a rescue league and began plans for the required home visit and fenced area. But a nagging thought kept surfacing: we should get a puppy, a girl we could raise and train from babyhood, who would know only us as her family. And the rescued dogs were almost exclusively older Danes at least a little affected by emotional or behavioral issues.

"How about a breeder?" my husband said.

I shook my head, thinking about all the dogs at shelters, the abandoned dog my mom had collected from the woods, and Sara's mother, tied to a telephone pole on a rural road days before giving birth. The next day a different rescue organization, one I'd never heard of, posted a puppy Dane for adoption. I sent the application. We were offered the dog the next morning.

In our marriage, I am the proactive planner. My husband is the patient voice of practicality. As I made lists of new puppy equipment and tried to locate a retailer for the dog food I'd researched, my husband quietly voiced a few concerns.

"Under what circumstances was the dog rescued? What does the $400 adoption fee cover? Are there any guarantees that this dog won't be sick within a few weeks? Who's the vet doing the spay, checkup, and shots?"

"Of course," I said. "I'll ask."

Unbelievably, when I called, the woman fostering the puppy snapped at me—"What do you need to know the name of the vet for?"—and could not produce valid answers. The next morning, she e-mailed and rejected us as potential adopters.

I felt tricked and hurt. Dee, a friend of mine who raises and shows Welsh corgis, told me that it was for the best, that the red flags were apparent, that occasionally some "rescues" are suspected of being extensions of puppy mills.

"What about a breeder?" Dee said.

I balked again. "I grew up watching my mother help homeless dogs and strays; I don't think I can do that. Besides, what breeder would want to sell me a dog? The first thing I'm going to do when the dog is old enough is have her spayed."

Dee explained the difference between show-quality and pet-quality puppies and how most breeders expected a puppy going to a pet home to be altered. In fact, it was usually a part of the required contract.

I realized then that I knew very little about the purchase of a pure-bred dog and wonder if perhaps I had been too hasty in eliminating that option. But I still thought a Great Dane pup would show up at a shelter, ready for rescue. After checking postings daily for weeks with no leads, however, I grew discouraged.

"What about a breeder?" my mother said. "You need a dog. Your house needs a dog. The boys need a dog to grow up with."

"Don't you think I should wait?"

"For what? You can rescue dogs once the boys aren't little anymore."

I grudgingly began to look at the websites my husband had bookmarked for me. "Start a dialogue with a few people," my husband suggested. With

Dee's mentorship and an increasing confidence in this path, I researched articles on breeders, assembled a list of questions, and filled out a few online questionnaires about our home and property.

A woman in an adjacent state e-mailed, saying she thought we had a "nice situation for one of her dogs," and I wrote a polite and cheerful response that incorporated six questions about temperament, health testing, and exposure to children. She e-mailed back a diatribe against health testing in pure-blooded large breeds. She also insisted that temperament in a puppy could not be assessed, but that her dogs had no animosity toward humans when they left her farm and that whatever happened after that would be "my problem, not hers." She also informed me that my six questions were more than she'd ever had to respond to before and that they clearly showed me to be both a "neatnik" and a "very insecure" dog owner.

What the heck was this? Every positive lead seemed to shift into a foreboding and murky signal to give up. But Dee told me that legitimate breeders would welcome questions; in fact, they would be thrilled to find someone who took the process seriously. I sighed and went back to the computer.

For a few more nights, I searched, read, and debated. I now considered only breeders listed on the Great Dane Club of America site and followed up with only those who were opposed to ear cropping. This left very few in a five-state radius. About to give up, I clicked on the last breeder's site in the last state. On a page of puppies, her photo was first: a beautiful mantle female with quiet brown eyes. I read every word on the site, and after learning that the breeder favored natural ears, I stayed up until 1:00 A.M. filling out the questionnaire.

When the breeder wrote back saying that she, too, had a preschool-age son and an eight-month-old baby, I suspected the quest was approaching the treasured end. We arranged to travel to Delaware on the way home from on a holiday weekend, and we planned to take the pup home that day.

I named her Zoe. On the breeder's living room floor, the puppy pulled at my scarf and tripped over her own enormous paws. When we left, she didn't want to be pulled along on a leash, unused to the sensation. So I picked her up, and she willingly settled her weight against my hip and side, trusting me inherently.

The driveway appears in the darkness, and our white house suddenly glows in the flood of our high beams. The baby quiets on his own, as if sensing the proximity of his crib and toys. My husband and I lift the puppy down to the cold ground. Once inside, she shakes off the five-hour drive and romps through the entryway and kitchen and back again. Her sweet, chocolatey eyes keep seeking me out. She weighs as much as Aidan, but she sniffs cabinets and explores corners like a curious toddler.

Aidan giggles and follows her. We will have lessons on puppy behavior and placement in the pack, how to carefully play with a Dane and how to let a pup alone when she tires. But for now his laugh keeps me still. Sara used to sniff his face when he would enter the house, and he would respond with that giggle. The sound of it fills the rooms again.

"Mommy, what's Zoe mean?" Aidan asks. He has been into names lately, considering the naming process and the significance of one's name. His means "fiery spirit"; mine means "white wave."

"It means 'life,'" I say.

Zoe bounds down the hall right into the kitchen island, bounces off, and keeps going. She seems to have accepted us—screaming baby and slippery floors and new smells and all. She turns and climbs onto my lap, legs and tail spilling everywhere, and I feel a bit of a lift. Not a total release, but enough to know that this dog is the right dog for us in this time and place, that this dog is the one who will complete us in the years to come.

—*Jenn Brisendine*

Wag the Dog

O kay. We didn't name the newest addition to our family Wag, although it did cross our inane minds. As did Jell-O, Jingles, Moxie, Max, Fluffy, Scruffy, Snowball, Sam, and Sid. The moniker of Nipper was also tossed around a good bit—given consideration primarily for the surprisingly accurate descriptive quality it possesses.

My husband, of course, lobbied hard for simply calling him Dog—born of a ludicrous and, thankfully, thwarted desire to name his cat Cat. (How completely juvenile!) But I digress.

After great deliberation, carefully weighing the appropriateness and popularity of each possibility, we finally settled on a name for the puppy that Santa, in his infinite wisdom and boundless generosity, bestowed upon us Christmas morning. In the end, Jack Snowflake garnered the most votes.

So it was: Jack—"because he popped out of a box like a jack-in-the-box, Mommy!" And Snowflake— "because he's fluffy and white like snow!"

But it was a compromise of sorts—in more ways than one. Not many of us in this household (myself included) actually wanted a pooch. But now that we have officially joined the ranks of "dog people," we're slowly warming to the notion, completely in love with his smallish bark and his I'm-a-big-ferocious-dog growl, which surfaces whenever he wrestles a sock into submission. Chief among the reasons for this unlikely development: Jack is so stinking adorable that it is beyond comprehension—almost to the point of edibleness. In a word, he's a quart-sized ball of cottony fluff that I am physically incapable of leaving alone. Nor can I resist the urge to coo to him like a new mother, convinced that her wriggling infant can actually understand the deluge of gibberish that spills from her unremittingly.

Yes, I talk to the damn dog. As if he were a sweet, sweet baby. We discuss happenings in this house, the goings and comings of its inhabitants, the gnaw-worthiness of his toys, the fleeciness of his blankie, the futility of nursing cats, assorted political hokum, and of course, poop.

"My, what a big boy you're getting to be, Jack! And what big teeth you have!" Without question, I have uttered this prideful phrase no less than forty-six times a week and have cheered his piddlings (when properly placed) at least that many times in the last three days alone—as have all who have witnessed said joyous achievements. Well, it certainly seems as if we've hooted and hollered over wee-wee success that often.

Further, the kiddos have invested a goodly chunk of time teaching our fuzzy friend a thing or two, cleverly demonstrating each in turn—like how to wave bye-bye, how to prance around on two paws, how to lie down so that a belly rub will result. They've even credited themselves with showing their beloved Snowflake how to bark, growl, and pant. Where, I ask, would he be without them? I shudder to think—considering that my husband and I would have likely halted instruction after he nailed the pooping-and-peeing-in-the-right-spot gig. Well, he sort of nailed it. Indeed, there is room for improvement. Lots of room.

Mostly, I think, the dog in question has failed to totally master the potty routine because he isn't particularly interested in seeing that I achieve my objective—getting him to relieve himself in a timely fashion in the appropriate location, with or without treats and an inordinate amount of cajoling. His objective, apparently, carries far more appeal—that which involves stumbling upon and inspecting (but, hopefully, not eating) all-that-is-completely-deplorable-and-dreadfully-repulsive on the face of the earth. Stuff like deer droppings, cigarette butts, wads of chewing gum, discarded Band-Aids, snippets of carrion, and of course, dog dung at all stages of decomposition. Each deserves an untold degree of scrutiny. His fuzzy snout, it seems, is keenly drawn to every speck of foulness that lurks in our path. The ranker the entity, the better in Jack's beady little eyes.

My function, apparently, is to plant myself at the end of the leash like a dutiful dolt, feigning both patience and understanding, until he is completely satisfied with having sniffed-to-death whatever it was that piqued his interest in the first place. As his loyal companion, I apparently am also expected to tolerate his sinfully erratic movements and delusions of grandeur that center around an unwavering belief that he is a draft horse on a mission to haul me into a neighboring county.

How an eight-pound ball of fluff can drag me anywhere is beyond me. But he does, and he's happy to do so, huffing and puffing, his tongue flapping all the way . . . to the next bit of repulsiveness. "Who knows," I reason, "maybe this will be the bit of repulsiveness that makes him deposit his own bit of repulsiveness!"

So, when we do finally decide to venture out into the world at large, I suppose it should be no surprise to me that the muttonhead acts like a deranged squirrel, skittering hither and yon in an absolute panic over the feast for the senses bestowed upon him. It's the ultimate canine smorgasbord, featuring a whole host of odoriferous items that simply must be classified somewhere on that hideous Stench Scale. Needless to say, I hold on tight, lest he yank my shoulder out of its socket.

As luck would have it, my charges often tag along for the festivities, scouring great patches of earth for evidence of poo. Shouts of "Fresh poopie alert, Mommy! Let Jack smell it quick!" can be heard far and wide.

And like any overly exuberant, newish parents, we've journeyed far and wide to purchase the latest and greatest gear to outfit him, dropping an inordinately large sum of cash for stuff we apparently think we'll need in the next decade—to include a glorified pen and expandable baby gates, roughly 16 million chew toys, a cushy bed (that's reversible!), a jazzy harness thingy, and a fancy-schmancy leash (that I have absolutely no trouble at all entwining around my legs). We even splurged on a natty little sweater and a doggie-wearing device, so that I can take him with me on longer jaunts around the neighborhood—calling his attention to all the lovely places to poop.

Good Lord, what's happened to me?

I'm embarrassed to admit that the tail may, in fact, be wagging the dog here. In retrospect, maybe Wag would have been a befitting name for our newest family member. Then again, I've been told I don't know Jack.

—*Melinda L. Wentzel*

Serendipity on Four Legs

"Come see my dog," Bodie drawled from his front porch, just a few yards from mine.

I followed him around back, where a squat but fully grown rottweiler sat chained to a rusty shed. She shrank back, hesitating before she sniffed my extended palm. Her coat glistened like freshly poured tar under the July sun. She obviously hadn't missed too many meals. Still, something about her shyness made me suspicious.

"Bodie, I don't think she's been treated very well."

"Name's Grady," he said. "A lady I did some work for gave her to me today. She's been letting Grady live on her porch but can't afford to feed her anymore. Her little boy was playing outside one day when a neighbor of theirs got hauled off to jail. As the cops handcuffed the guy, he hollered to the boy,

'Take care of my dog!' That's how they ended up with her. Got her for Brayden."

Bodie's eight-year-old son visited every other weekend. I wondered if Grady could win the boy's heart from his full-time dog at his mom's house. I was skeptical, but couldn't blame Bodie for trying.

"Well, you can't leave her chained up like this."

But Bodie did leave Grady chained up like that. It surprised me. He was an honest man. He worked hard and helped his neighbors. Keeping a chained rottweiler in the middle of the city didn't seem like something he'd do.

As his personal problems mounted, Bodie was home less and less, and Grady was alone, chained to the shed, more and more. Every day after work I brought her fresh water. I wondered whether she'd ever seen the inside of a veterinary clinic or a home. So I took Grady to my house in the evenings. She'd nudge my hand, demanding more behind-the-ear scratches. While she gobbled up the attention, she vibrated with a low growl, like an approaching thunderstorm. "Grumbling" the breed books called it. I called it her purr.

She romped with our six-month-old chocolate Lab, Zoe. Both dogs, my husband, and I were in a heated game of tug-of-war late one night when the phone rang.

"You got my dog?" Bodie asked.

"Yeah, we've got her," I said and handed the phone to my husband.

"You need to do the right thing, Bodie, and let us keep her," he said.

Ten minutes and another phone call later, and Grady was ours. It was her fourth home in what we guessed was her first year or two of life.

Grady nuzzled into our lives as if we'd raised her from birth. She was an eager driving companion and a spry running partner, setting the pace and lapping up the water I squirted from my bottle at stoplights.

Within a few months, the four of us started a new life 25 miles away, where the suburbs met the country. Grady thrived there. She and Zoe traipsed through woods behind our house. As much as Grady loved our acre-and-a-half yard, she wasn't above fence-jumping in hot pursuit of something, usually a herd of deer. She'd turn up a short time later, lounging at the end of our driveway, waiting for one of us to bring her inside. Occasionally, she'd wait us out on a neighbor's porch.

Grady especially loved the shallow river nearby. She'd fetch whatever we threw in and drudge up treasures from the river bed. Her favorite was a small wagon wheel she worked at least twenty minutes to unearth. After we assured a passing kayaker that the quirky rottweiler was harmless, Grady swam behind him, nipping the back of the plastic boat like it was something else she wanted for her collection of goodies.

She could be a bit obsessive. Once, I waded waist-deep into a mucky pond to drag her out before she drowned. Grady had exhausted herself swimming after Canadian geese that had interrupted another game of water fetch. Zoe, usually the less obedient of the two, happily gave up the chase and joined me on the bank when I called. But Grady seemed like she'd rather drown than give up. She struggled to keep her head above water but never took her eyes off the geese.

Throughout my first pregnancy, Grady mirrored my every flinch. If I leaned left, she did too. If I took one step back, she did too. If I curled up on the couch, she did too. I don't think Grady knew what to make of my son when he arrived, though. He fell into her category of "things that move and make noise." Such things, like the vacuum cleaner, annoyed her. The infant seemed more to perplex her. Whereas Grady would bark, lunge, and bite at the running vacuum cleaner, she'd squeak, nudge, and lick my son's head when I carried him.

As our son grew, he and Grady became play-mates. It delighted them both when Grady chased and chomped after bubbles and balloons. By the time my son was in first grade, Grady was probably twelve.

One Saturday, my son and I left Grady pondering her reflection in our swimming pool while we drove his overnight guest home. On the way back, it started raining. Cars in both lanes slammed on their brakes and swerved to keep from hitting a little dog in the road. I pulled over and opened my door. Before I could step out, in leaped a Jack Russell terrier. He had no collar, but the dog's white fur was clean despite the rain, so I figured it must have a good home nearby. I stopped people walking by and knocked on several doors, but no one recognized the dog.

"I thought it must be yours," said one elderly gentleman, "when we saw it jump into your car like that. My wife has been trying to catch the little thing, but it kept running from her."

I knocked on a few more doors before the rain became a downpour and I gave up.

"Let's take her home," I told my son. "We'll call the shelter and post some signs."

The shelter gave me several phone numbers of people who'd recently reported missing Jack Russells. Most of them believed their dogs had been stolen right out of their yards.

"Bring photo," I added to the dog-found flier. I wasn't about to hand her over to a thief. We were getting attached. Every time I sat down, she jumped into my lap.

"I feel like she's trying to tell me something," I told my husband.

He rolled his eyes. "Her owner's probably a woman." That night when we went to bed, the Jack Russell burrowed under the covers between us.

"Someone is missing her. I can feel it," I told my husband.

It was dark, but I think I heard his eyes roll again.

The next morning I posted signs, my new little friend in tow. I'd just hung the second sign in a neighborhood convenience store near where I'd found her. My cell phone rang before I'd hung the third dog-found notice.

"You found a dog? A Jack Russell?" a man said with a twang.

"Yes," I hesitated. If anyone's stealing dogs, I bet it's this guy, I thought.

"Does she get real excited when you call her Millie?" Out of the all the names we'd hurled at the dog the last 24 hours, Millie wasn't one of them. I tested it.

"Millie? Are you Millie?"

Her ears perked up. She wagged her tail. Exactly the same way she responded when my son called her "Jack," "Jackie," "Spot," "Zippy," and dozens of other names.

"I don't know," I told the potential dog thief. "Do you have a photo?"

"I've got one right here. You can see her pretty good. I'm still at the Quick Stop. Can you bring her up here now?"

"I'm just down the street."

I turned the car around and assured "Millie" that I'd never give her up to any unsavory characters. I pulled around the store and parked next to the extended cab pickup truck with the man standing beside it. This had to be the guy with the twang: work boots, worn jeans, faded T-shirt, dirty cap.

I backed out of my seat to keep the dog from escaping. I turned to ask the man for his photo, but he spoke first.

"Rebecca?"

It took a second to sink in.

"Bodie?"

We hugged.

"I can't believe that you, of all people, found Millie." He handed me the picture of a dog that was undoubtedly the one in my car right now—the one yipping and wagging her tail.

Warily, I let Millie out of my car. She sprang into Bodie's arms and licked his face.

"My wife's been torn up about losing Millie. We'd just given her a bath when she slipped out and ran off. You gotta come meet my wife. I've told her all about you and Grady. She's never going to believe this. We live just down the street. Follow me home."

"You bet I will."

We pulled into the driveway, and Bodie pointed out his Harley in the garage. "I'm doing good now. I own a rent house too. Workin' a lot. Got another baby comin' in January."

He let Millie in the door first, and I followed Bodie inside. I met his wife and their other dog, a rat terrier named Killer. The dogs were clearly cared for and loved here in this tidy, well-decorated ranch house just three miles from mine.

We talked about Grady and the old neighborhood. We marveled at how our paths crossed again— 25 miles, ten years, and two dogs from where we'd first met.

A few hours later, Grady had a seizure, her first since I'd had her. I was stunned because her vet had given her a clean bill of health just a couple of weeks before. Grady died that night of slow-growing tumors no one knew she had.

A strange thought struck me as I cried. On Grady's last day of life, both of Bodie's dogs were in my home at the same time. Found ten years apart, one I'd rescued from him, the other for him. I wonder if Grady died knowing her loose ends were tied up. She'd have liked that.

—Rebecca Sims

Some names have been changed to provide the privacy of those individuals.

For Dog's Sake!

When your kids go off to college, they leave behind so many things. I could fully stock a PTA thrift store with what they left in their wake. But one thing left behind stays put—their childhood pet.

So Bubba, my son's golden retriever, spent his days roaming the confines of our yard. Nightly, he hunkered down inside our garage.

Bubba was lonely. Days when landscapers mowed and blowed were like fiesta time for Bubba. Those were happy days, too, when the gas meter guy came. Bubba took a real shine to his leg. The meter reader hobbled to his truck with our dog still molesting his leg. Contrary to his affectionate behavior toward the gas guy was the way he treated the electricity meter lady, who cussed him and snarled back.

Bubba's favorite visitors became the dogs walked past our yard with long leashes, allowing them to nuzzle him. Bubba could schmooze with these pooches on his turf without getting a jolt. Stung once in the first few days after the electric fence's installation, he quivered spasmodically, jumping into the air and yelping in pain. What dog wouldn't?

When I retrieved the paper yesterday, Bubba rolled over, and I rubbed his belly. Later, I saw Bubba trotting around the pool. About noon, I heard him barking. I called him, grabbed his collar, and held on till the meter gal departed hastily. Next, I spied him following the leaf blowers. I was cleaning out my refrigerator at the time. When I went out to feed him scraps, I caught Bubba chewing some newly planted bushes. I returned inside to get ready for my optician appointment. With my elderly father in tow, I locked the back door.

Dad pointed down the steps. "What's the matter with your dog?" Bubba was shaking uncontrollably. I scanned the sky. Thunder? Nope. It was another Carolina blue, cloudless, autumn day. I patted Bubba. His body convulsed more. The whites of his eyes blazed red. He could hardly walk. I opened the hatch of our 4 Runner and hoisted the shaking dog inside.

"We're going to the vet!"

Now, Bubba couldn't stand. He lay convulsing spasmodically, his breathing labored.

Usually, Dad's incessant chatter, nonstop jokes, and repetitions of anecdotes from his youth roll off my back, but yesterday my nerves were shot. I feared losing my son's best friend.

I zoomed into the parking lot of the veterinary clinic.

"Wait here!" I ordered Dad and ran inside.

Folks jawboning at the counter made me want to scream, "I have a very sick dog that can't wait on pleasantries!" But I didn't. I bit my lip. I shifted my weight. I looked anxiously toward my hatchback.

Finally, I spoke up: "Dying dog coming through!"

While I strained as I carried my trembling canine into an examining room, the vet walked in. She quickly shaved the dog's paw and began drawing blood. Her assistant hooked up the IV while I shook.

"It looks like poison," said the vet. "We'll do a toxicology report." She peered over her glasses at me. "Did you put out fertilizer?"

"No."

"Do you put Sevin Dust on your dog?"

"No."

"Flea medication?"

"He's got fleas?"

"Did you use it?"

"No."

"Is he up to date on his shots?"

"I think so," I lied.

"Heartworm pills?"

"Not now. No mosquitoes in November."

"We'll keep him overnight." She looked hard at me. "Does he roam?"

"No."

"Is he spayed?"

"No." I answered.

She frowned while I pictured Bubba intently humping the meter man's leg.

"Spaying will protect him from prostrate troubles," informed the vet. "Any chemicals around?"

"My husband cleaned the pool. He uses chlorine pucks. I thought I collected all the chlorine shards from the backyard. Dang his obsessive-compulsive cleanliness streak—"

She interrupted my rant. "I don't think it's chlorine poisoning."

"The meter gal from the electric company doesn't like my dog."

"Hmm," murmured the vet.

I left Bubba with the vet and trekked over to my husband's medical office. I recounted all the scenarios. He particularly fastened on the nefarious metermaid theory. "Should I call the electric company?"

"Wait on that," he cautioned.

I called the energy company, anyway. "Has anybody else's dog become violently ill after a meter reading?" I asked.

"No, Ma'am," answered an amused person.

"It wasn't the mean meter maid," I told my husband. And then a light bulb exploded in my head! I put my hands to my temples; my voice cracked. "It was me! I've killed Bubba!" I blubbered.

"Huh?" said my husband.

"Moldy cheese!"

"What?"

"I gave him moldy cheese. I cleaned out the fridge and fed him moldy cheese." I began to cry.

"That wouldn't do it. Most likely it's a bacterial infection."

I sobbed. "It's the moldy cheese. It's my fault."

My husband called me at home later.

"The vet gave Bubba charcoal," he said.

"Charcoal? Is that a New-Age cure?"

"She gave him diazepam to sedate him and activated charcoal to absorb the toxins."

The next morning I phoned the vet. My voice trembled. "Is Bubba alive?"

"Oh, yes!" came the cheery response.

"Great!"

"You can pick him up today."

"Wow! You know, Doctor, last night I remembered I gave Bubba moldy cheese."

There was a pause. "I have an article I'll give you when you come," she said.

Dad and I scrambled to go get our dog. I paid the bill, and out came Bubba—a new, greatly improved version of the dog I had left there yesterday.

The doctor handed me a sheet of paper. It read: "Sources of tremorgenic mycotoxins for household pets have included moldy dairy foods, moldy walnuts or peanuts, stored grains, and moldy spaghetti." I looked into the vet's eyes. "Thank you," I whispered.

Bubba jumped into our car. I closed the hatch, got in, and turned to Dad.

"Guess how much those four ounces of moldy Philadelphia Cream Cheese cost me?" I asked.

"A hundred bucks."

"Try four times that!"

My frugal dad whistled and then patted Bubba on the head. "Money well spent," he declared.

"From now on, Bubba eats only what we eat!"

"We'll be his food testers!"

"Yeah, boy! Better for us to fall ill. It's cheaper for us to get sick than Bubba."

—Erika Hoffman

My Perfect Nursemaid

One cheerful sunny morning I stood in the backyard under the washline, faced with overflowing baskets of wet laundry. Eight months pregnant with my fifth child, I felt cumbersome and frequently exhausted and was waiting impatiently for the baby's arrival.

My two eldest children were at school, but the two younger boys, Bruce and Timm, still too young for school, were at home. Sturdy and healthy, Bruce and Timm were close companions who looked so alike, with their blonde hair and grey eyes, that they were often mistaken for twins. The backyard was their country. There, they pulled cardboard box carts, raced dinky cars, threw balls, and played imaginary games. They were happy children, content with each other's company.

I was filled with maternal love as I watched my boys rolling in the grass, giggling, talking their personal language, and tumbling like puppies. Circling round them, snuffling and grunting, was their steadfast friend, Honey.

"Hallo, boys," I called.

"Hi, Ma," I dimly heard in reply. They were so engrossed in their play that their mother had receded into a shadowy background figure.

"Honey! Honey!" I called, clapping my hands.

Our dog blundered toward me, circled around, and then scuttled back to the boys, where the fun was.

I had acquired her under trying circumstances. When my fourth child arrived, my other children had measles. The doctor insisted the new baby stay in safety at the maternity hospital. My ever-impractical mother, worried that I would return home empty-handed, presented me with a bulldog puppy.

The pup was a bundle of honey-colored loose skin with such a beguiling nature that she would be sure to delight any child. However, with three sick children and a new baby, a puppy, which would need constant attention, was not the most rational or practical present to give a young mother. What I needed was a nursemaid!

Bruce, then only eighteen months old, was nonplussed as he silently scrutinized what he thought was his new brother. However, he soon realized that his new playmate was more exciting than the new baby I eventually brought home. The puppy played; the baby slept. As the months passed, my two young sons and the puppy formed a bond of protective friendship.

Honey soon became our self-designated security guard. When the children rested after lunch she would guard the house. Her place was on the front porch, where she kept a constant watch on passersby. Usually, upon seeing what they thought was a ferocious bulldog, they crossed to the other side of the road. If Honey thought they came too close, the occasional growl would surface from deep within her barrel chest—just a warning to keep a safe distance.

Humming the latest popular tunes for inspiration, I watched the trio engrossed in play for a few moments before turning my attention to the mound of washing. The smell of jasmine floated heady and sensuous as I slowly bent and stretched, hanging line after line of never-ending laundry. I was soon mesmerized by the warmth of the day and my own monotonous singing. I drifted into a trance, forgetting everything outside of the eternal washing.

I placed the last peg on the last shirt, stopped humming, turned to pick up the baskets . . . and suddenly realized that silence had enveloped the yard. No giggling boys. No yelping dog. My eyes quickly darted around the yard. No children. No bulldog. I panicked.

"Bruce! Timm! Honey!" I shouted.

Not a sound. Dropping the baskets, I quickly moved into the house and searched every room, hoping they were playing inside. No sign of anyone. Toys lay strewn, stillborn, waiting for the boys to breathe life into them. Surely they couldn't have escaped from the house. The front door was always locked. I stumbled into the hallway. The always-locked front door was now unlocked and open; so was the front gate. I was frightened and anxious. Moaning with exertion, I staggered out of the gate, scanning the road ahead.

Although we lived in a quiet cul-de-sac, it led to a busy main road that ran past the airport. Shaking with despair, I swept the scene ahead with my eyes. Way in the distance, I discerned the three truants making their way toward the dangerous highway.

Hands protecting my unborn bulge, I lumbered toward the distant figures. I was scared to shout, in case they thought it was a game and ran away from me. No, I had to entice them to turn around. My brain raced with ideas. I must offer them something they couldn't resist. Food! That was sure to do it.

Before I had time to think clearly, I was jolted back to the scene ahead as I noticed Honey's behavior. Bulldogs don't normally bark, but I distinctly heard menacing snarls and barks as she positioned herself in front of the boys, jumping up, trying to make them turn back. As they moved closer to danger, the threatening growls grew louder as Honey displayed her fiercest and most intimidating weapon, her teeth.

Hanging onto each other, the children stopped at the edge of the road and screamed. Disoriented and lost, frightened by Honey's unfamiliar behavior, they clung together. Honey stood her ground, barking incessantly at the boys, frozen in alarm. Their friend had turned into a snarling monster.

The baby, sensing my fear, was agitated, arms and legs protesting. I sobbed in prayer as high-powered trucks lurched past, belching evil-smelling diesel fumes. At last, I was within calling distance.

"Lunch time!" I shouted.

They turned. Thank God. I had caught their attention.

"Chocolate ice cream!" I yelled.

Their faces lit up in disbelief.

I knew they deserved punishment, but that might have sent them scuttling into the danger zone. So I swallowed my instinctive tongue-lashing and called again with arms outspread to embrace the little devils. It worked. Rather than face a ferocious bulldog, they ran to me, where chocolate ice cream was offered.

Safe. I held them close. With tears close to the surface, I turned to pat their rescuer.

Honey's whole body quivered with expectation. She knew she'd done something worthy of my love and attention. Her silky ears were fluttering with anticipation. Her eyes sparkled, while her tongue lolled long and dripping. Snuffling and grunting, she waited for the reward she knew she deserved.

Awkwardly, I bent to fondle her wrinkled forehead murmuring, "What a clever girl. What a brave dog. Oh, thank you, thank you."

Her smile stretched from ear to ear. Her undershot jaw with its terrorist teeth was to me her greatest asset. She was the most beautiful dog.

As we slowly made our way home to safety and chocolate ice cream, I pondered life's oddities. What I had thought to be the height of my mother's impractical presents had turned out to be the most practical. Honey was not only a playmate for my children and a watch dog for our home. She had also turned out to be the perfect nursemaid I had so ardently desired.

—*Ann Hoffman*

All in the Family

When Ray and I married, we blended our families of adult children. Committed to the idea that we also needed a child together to bind us, I looked around for a good candidate and found Annie, an eighty-pound, two-year old golden retriever.

"What do you think?" I asked Ray when I brought her home.

"Big. Very big." Ray eyed her suspiciously but agreed to keep her, making every effort to please, as new husbands often do.

My period of bonding with Annie lasted two seconds. No living thing smiles as broadly and leans against one's leg as sweetly as a golden retriever. If that golden is tall enough to rest her nose on the countertop, has splendid feathers on her legs and tail, and is the color of a new penny, all the better.

Ray needed longer, but Annie won him over with her soft eyes, sunny disposition and her eagerness to be with us both at all times. After several months he greeted her daily with, "There's my dog, Annie," as he tousled her fur and she thumped her tail against his leg.

But we had a few kinks to work out. One day Ray found me in the bathroom lathering Annie in our tub. "How do you like the frosted look?" I asked, swirling froth into white curls on her head. I thought he'd be very pleased since he'd mentioned Annie's natural body odor getting a bit ripe.

"You're bathing her in our bathtub?" He didn't sound pleased at all.

"I've always bathed my dogs in the tub," I assured him. "I scrub it out afterward."

"And clog the drainpipes with all that hair?"

I didn't want any arguments over Annie, so I refrained from explaining that I'd bathed four golden retrievers in my tub over the years and not clogged one pipe. Instead, I promised to work grooming into the joint house budget every few months.

Then there was the kink when I loaded Annie in the back seat of our Honda Accord.

"She'll get dirt and hair everywhere," Ray said. "That towel you have on the back seat won't begin to cut it."

I solved that problem by replacing the Accord with a slate-gray Prius. I put the back seat down, filled the elevated cargo area with three large, washable, fleece-covered foam pads, and invited Annie to jump in. Ray delighted in the dramatically improved gas mileage of the Prius. Annie delighted in the opportunity to stretch out full-length in total comfort, to rest nose on paws, and to watch the world go by, eyes level with the windows.

Our lives settled into a pleasant routine that has continued for nine years now. Every morning, as soon as I venture into the kitchen, Annie takes a sentinel stand beside her stainless-steel bowl. *Did you forget to give me breakfast?* she seems to say.

I pat her head, then fill her bowl with two scoops of kibbles, a vitamin, and a glucosamine supplement. After gulping down her food in less time than it takes me to make a cup of tea and a piece of toast, she follows me to my home office, where I settle at my desk and she plops down on her beanbag dog bed.

When Ray gets up, usually an hour or two later, Annie scrambles to her feet and rushes to greet him.

"Get it, girl," Ray says, and I hear her barrel down the hall after one of her toys.

After she or Ray tires of the game, Annie returns to my office and takes a little nap while Ray eats breakfast and I tweak an essay. A half hour or so later, she wakes up, stretches in a perfect yoga downward dog pose, and comes to my desk, pushing her nose under my arm. I pat her head, then she pads out of the room.

I sigh, take a last glance at my story in progress, and push the "save" button on my computer. "I'd rather not go right now," I mutter, but I know Annie is standing at the front door. It's time for our morning walk, she reminds us. It's a good thing, story-in-progress notwithstanding. Because of her, we get our daily exercise, rain, shine, and even, occasionally, snow.

I gather a leash and a plastic bag and tuck a bottle of water and collapsible dog bowl into my fanny pack.

"Thanks for getting us out, girl," Ray tells Annie, stroking her back before he puts on his shoes, pockets the house key, and we head out the door.

As we walk through our neighborhood of late 1970s split-level homes and well-kept yards or head to the field by a nearby elementary school, we often see neighbors walking their dogs. *We've got to stop and socialize,* I know Annie is thinking. She and the other dogs sniff and circle each other, nose to tail, or run ragged circles while we owners chat. Because of Annie, Ray has met new golf buddies and I've met some fellow writers.

Sometimes we replace our walk with a hike in nearby Tryon Creek State Park. Annie bounds up trails bordered by maples, hemlocks, and firs, wild with excitement. But after just minutes, she takes her self-appointed place between Ray and me, her head swiveling like a bobble head from me to Ray and back to me as she trods along, implying, *You're both here, right? We're family, you know. We must stay together.*

Plans for the Fourth of July and New Year's Eve have included Annie since the night I awoke to fireworks and a *thunk* on my chest. I opened my eyes and looked right into Annie's face, two paws on me, two paws still on the floor. Firecrackers hissed and screamed somewhere down the street. The message was clear: *Can I crawl in bed with you 'til those scary things stop? Please?*

There are, of course, those times when Ray and I can't take Annie with us. If we don our bicycling clothes, the luster in Annie's eyes pales and she sinks dejectedly onto the rug. When we return, she bounds to us, quivering with joy.

But when Ray and I pull out suitcases to pack for a weekend out of town, she's sure she can come along. She presses her damp nose into our palms and looks up with eyes that beg, *Do they have a dog-friendly hotel where you're going?*

"You can go, girl," Ray says without my asking. She does belong on family outings, after all, and a lot of places welcome pets these days.

Annie's unfailing devotion has helped Ray and me get through some tough times. The day we came home from burying Ray's father and the day we returned from sitting with Ray's mother as she transitioned from this life, I laid on the floor beside Annie and buried my head in her soft belly, comforted by her warmth. *I care about what you are going through*, she seemed to say. *You'll all be okay.*

Should Ray and I argue within earshot of Annie, she promptly comes to sit by one of us, then the other, looking us both in the eye, scolding, *Look, you guys, knock it off. This family is about love.*

Recently, two things occurred to threaten our domestic tranquility. Both the economy and Annie's hind end nearly folded. I knew I couldn't do anything about the economy, but I hoped I could do something about Annie.

X-rays showed she had no hip dysplasia or masses. Her senior profile indicated nothing unusual. The veterinarian suggested we try acupuncture for general flexibility.

Ray and I are believers in acupuncture, but it would be an added expense at a difficult time. I expected Ray to say no. He worries about money when the market is up, let alone when it's tumbling. Instead, he said, "There'll never be another dog like Annie."

"Acupuncture costs a lot less than surgery, if she'd need that," I pointed out. "We could cancel our ski trip to cover the expense and then some." Images from the brochure about our planned trip to Whistler flashed in my mind. I'd always wanted to go there. But I couldn't enjoy any ski run as much as I enjoyed Annie.

Acupuncture helped enormously for several months. Then Annie again began to walk stiff-legged with her tail tucked between her legs. This time the vet recommended we try physical therapy. A physical therapist for Annie? The stock market was still going down. Where would we draw the line?

Drawing the line on an animal's care is a very personal decision. I wouldn't think of making it for anyone else. Some people view their animals as, well, animals. Others view them as members of the family. Furthermore, in many cases expensive care for pets simply isn't an option. In our case, we decided we could shuffle priorities for our only child still living at home. Ray and I sat at the dining room table with notepads and pens to budget, Annie stretched at our feet.

"We can do a smaller Christmas for each other this year," I said. "We can drop the thermostat two degrees and bundle up more."

"We can eat out less often. We both make healthier dinners at home, anyway," Ray said. "And we can put concerts and plays on hold for a while."

The physical therapist diagnosed Annie's hind-end problem as a twisted pelvis. Manipulation and massage aligned her spine, laser treatments reduced the inflammation, and hydrotherapy plus exercises we did at home built muscle strength and endurance. The success of her treatments amazed us.

We've been very fortunate that we could help our girl. This morning we're off to the school again. Yesterday we had a beautiful hike in Tryon Creek.

"She's a dog, for gosh sakes," a friend said when she heard of Annie's regimen.

Maybe in some people's minds. But to us she's family.

—*Samantha Ducloux Waltz*

Blackie's Gift

Our woodland Montana home shares a clearing with more than a dozen white tail deer. Every year, does give birth in the woods behind our house. We've seen fawns so young their legs still wobble and marveled as a fawn became first a doe, then a mother herself. Our first set of twins has matured into the Buck Brothers—two sturdy fellows whose racks boast four points to a side and who loll away summer afternoons under the lilacs in the side yard.

But the most astonishing deer sighting was a gift from our Border collie, Blackie. She and her sister Whitey, a mismatched pair from the same litter, were unplanned puppies, gifts from a rancher who lived down the road from the weathered farmhouse where I lived when I first came back to my native state. An energetic pup who delighted in romping with my other dogs and teasing the two cats, Blackie grew into a gentle sweetheart with classic Border-collie coloring, except for her face. Instead of the traditional black with a vertical white line down the forehead to the nose, hers was split in two, half black and half white. It made her look like she was asking a question: *When can we play? When can we go for a walk? Will you love me forever, like I'll love you?*

When playtime was over and we all settled inside, Blackie often slept on top of the old furnace grate, snoring gently, or sat by my chair as I read, the top of her head fit perfectly into the cup of my hand.

But she'd been born to ranching stock and her herding instinct was strong. Barely past pocket-sized, she and Whitey worked a hundred-pound German shepherd into the corner of the sprawling farmhouse yard in minutes, leaving the bigger dog bewildered and its owner and me laughing. One wintry day, when a young steer wandered from my neighbor's pasture and I couldn't reach the rancher by phone, Blackie and I took the steer home. Though she'd never been trained to work cattle, she nipped and urged and directed the poor lost thing right where he needed to go.

That ability to keep things moving became even more important when my marriage ended and I found myself alone in the isolated farmhouse with five young animals. Some mornings, only the need to feed the dogs dragged me out of bed and into some sort of routine. I was listless, wounded, and had lost my sense of direction. But Blackie kept me going. We took long walks through field and forest, up mountain trails and down the rutted two-tracks that ran beside the irrigation canals. Even when a whitetail ran across our path, tempting the other dogs to give chase, Blackie often lagged behind to keep me company. People in the community knew me by my dogs, and the man who read the electric meter brought them biscuits. We were a family.

A few years later, I remarried, to a man who loved my furry companions as much as I did. The gang and I moved to the town where Don lived, and we all settled into a new house deep in the woods. Just a few days after the move, the dogs and I went out exploring on the narrow dirt road that wound past the house and up into the hills. When we returned home, I sat on the weathered brick steps and patted their heads, first one, then the second, then the third, then back and forth at random, my hand rounded like the walnut cupping the stone in a shell game.

Then my hand found a lump on Blackie's shoulder, about the size of a ping pong ball. Hard, wiggly, new, not painful to her. But painful to me because I knew immediately that it wasn't right.

Though I hadn't had the chance to meet the local vet yet, she fit us in first thing the next morning. After examining her new patient, the vet got the same look on her face that I'd had in my heart and rearranged her surgery schedule.

Blackie was the first of my little crew to be seriously ill, but our worry turned to laughter when Blackie let us know that the red T-shirt we'd put on her to keep her from working on the stitches did not suit her style. Neither did the white shirt nor the green one. I knew then that her legendary Border-collie energy was back and that she'd make a perfect recovery.

She did, and the little dogs set about exploring our new landscape as thoroughly as they had our former homestead. Even the glaucoma that developed in Blackie's right eye didn't slow her down. Eventually, a bleed led to its removal and the discovery of cancer. Blackie adapted to life with one eye with all the determination she'd shown when boxing that German shepherd into the corner and escorting the lost steer back to pasture. She listed slightly as she ran, her head turned to give her a better line of sight. And she no longer cared to bushwhack, where heavy growth, fallen logs, and broken branches made the woods she loved hard to navigate. My fingertips brushed her head as we stuck to the trails, each of us contented. She showed no other signs of the disease, though, for more than a year, until one morning, she simply woke up very ill.

Within days, we knew Blackie would not recover. One night, Don took her outside for a few minutes before bed. She'd begun to wander, no longer certain of her surroundings or her routine, so he put her on a leash and let her lead him. Had she not been ill—had her senses been communicating with her brain—she would never have drawn him to the meadow in front of the house. There, in the light of a late June evening, curled up tightly and nestled in the tall grass, lay a tiny, newborn fawn.

Don hustled Blackie into the house and took me out for a peek. The fawn was almost luminescent. Wrapped in the fading light, it looked embryonic, perfect, so still we feared it might be dead. Though I could have watched for hours, we knew not to linger. The doe was nowhere in sight, but if she picked up our scent, she—like many other wild animals— might have chosen to abandon her baby.

The next morning, we went out early to check on the deer. We found the hollow where the fawn had lain. Next to it, a larger impression showed where the doe had settled in. Sleeping or watching? Most likely, she'd felt comfortable leaving the fawn alone in the meadow while she foraged because many nighttime predators shy away from open spaces. To the doe, the tall grass—so open and inviting to our dying dog—felt safe.

A few days later, the time came for us to let Blackie go. All that summer, the doe and fawn passed through the clearing. When I mowed the meadow, I left their beds untouched. The fawn grew steady and tall, racing with the other fawns, nipping at the older deer, sniffing my flower beds.

It's been several years now since we saw that shimmering fawn curled up in the long grass. I can no longer tell which doe among the families that roam these woods was that babe. But each spring, when the wild newborns begin to make their first appearances, I'm reminded of that magical late-night discovery and of how one little black and white dog helped me find my way again.

—Leslie Budewitz

The Dog Who Knew My Name

We were always beagle people. For twenty-five years, an assortment of beagles occupied a branch on the family tree and among them were many characters. Some were much loved and some not so much. We had Sparky, Muffett, Blue, and others I can't remember. But somewhere between the demise of one beagle and the first poop-free yard in years, the springer spaniel invasion began. This was a turn I was not in favor of. You see, I was beginning to like taking stress-free walks in that clean lawn. And can I tell you how nice it was to go away with no dog-sitting problems to confront?

Then one summer evening a friend of our oldest son walked through the kitchen door with a big "Hello" and a dog named Gracie on a lead. Nobody was more surprised than me. We didn't generally encourage people to bring their pets along when they

visited. Unbeknownst to me, however, was the conspiracy behind the visit. This dog was not owned by
the friend. He was bringing a dog to us out of his
and my sons' shared sympathy for our dogless state
and because Gracie was a rescue dog, courtesy of the
Springer Spaniel Rescue Society.

As the sad story of Gracie's elderly owner's plight
unfolded, I had a chance to examine the animal.
Fat but clean. Housetrained, female (spayed), and
friendly. My husband hinted that we might consider
taking the dog into our home. I wasn't loving the
idea, but I gave my assent when I realized a prior
"trial period" had been arranged without my knowledge. What's a girl to do?

The upshot of the conspiracy was that the trial
period went well and we had another dog, one distinctly different from our beagles. I mean, this dog was
actually smart. Being female, she had a preference for
my husband, but I was able to gain ground with her in
several areas when it came to food and extra petting.
In her estimation, though, the new hierarchy in the
family went something like this: MAN, Dog, woman.
But we got along and Gracie became our constant
companion. She also became a hero to us in a way
that would have made Timmy and Lassie proud.

Our barn is big, red, and old. As all old buildings
eventually do, ours needed a new roof one summer.

Our three grown sons, a few of their friends, and my husband set themselves to the task one hot August weekend. It was decided that a tin roof would be the best and cheapest way to go. Materials were delivered, tools were gathered, and the job got underway. Gracie dutifully followed her master wherever he went, sitting at the bottom of the ladder, attending him when he took breaks, and generally keeping an eye on his whereabouts. There were scary moments. Tin roofs are loads of fun to put up until the last few pieces are set to go on. There's not a whole lot to hold onto at that point, and those darn things are slippery. But with good humor and determination, the deed was accomplished—except for the tarring around the chimney.

This part my darling husband decided to tackle many days later when all his helpful companions had returned to their own busy lives—all, that is, but Gracie. After supper on that fateful evening, she watched him climb the thirty-foot ladder, tar bucket and rope in hand, brush at the ready. She watched him ascend the roof: slip, slide, slip. Then she watched him sling the rope around the chimney and suddenly stop. Unfortunately, he'd landed himself too far away from the chimney, and any slackening of the rope would have meant a calamity of Laurel and Hardy proportions. Tar boy in space.

I was in the kitchen doing the dishes when I heard the barking. The barn is a few hundred feet from the house with a long driveway and trees in between. At first I thought Gracie had cornered another chipmunk under the woodpile. But the barking got closer, and soon she was at the back door. *Was she thirsty?* I opened the door to let her in, but she looked up at me and headed back for the yard.

Dumb dog, I thought.

In seconds, she was back at the door again barking furiously. This time I went outside to have a look around. That's when I heard a weak "Help." So did Gracie, and more frantic barking ensued. Her eyes pleaded with me, and she took off for the barn.

As I got closer, I heard my husband. "Go get her, Gracie! Go get Sue!"

When I rounded the corner of the building and looked up, there he was, stuck with a heavy tar bucket in one hand and a firm grip on the rope too-far-from-the-chimney with the other.

"Good dog, Gracie," came triumphantly from the rooftop.

I couldn't believe what had just happened and bent down to give our dog a hug.

"Hey, up here," said Husband. "Grab this other end, would you?"

I grabbed the loose end of the rope that hung near the ladder and held it firmly as my thankful husband walked across the roof line to the chimney. He could now tar away.

Gracie gloried in our praise for weeks. I think it may also have been the beginning of her nightly spoonful of vanilla ice cream.

I'm so glad that no real terror awaited me that evening as I headed out the kitchen door to the barn. Husband was alive and well on the roof. But he would have been totally stuck and extremely aggravated if he'd not had Gracie to assist him.

Gracie and I became great friends, and I'm still astounded that she knew my name and where to find me in a crisis. The tin-roof rescue has also become one of our favorite family stories. The years we enjoyed Gracie's company also made it possible for us to take ownership of our second rescue springer spaniel, Libby, after the passing of Gracie. So I guess it must be said that we're not beagle people anymore, but I sure hope we don't need a new barn roof any time soon.

—*Susan Sundwall*

Christofur's Christmas

No matter how much my husband would riff upon the saintliness of his childhood Spots and Rovers, he hadn't a hope of convincing me that dogs were anything but evolved wolves waiting to devolve. It was 1957, and when Bob would invite me to watch the hit series *Lassie* with him, I would just sniff and go into the bedroom to read a book until the show was over. No canine heroics for me, thanks.

I knew better. Ever since I was ten, I'd been deathly afraid of dogs, and with good cause. Our neighbors had taken a weekend trip, cooping up their cocker spaniel in the garage while they were away. They asked me to go over in the morning to replenish his bowls of food and water, and I agreed, eager to earn a quarter. At the time, Scooter, graying around the chest and already rheumy-eyed, seemed harmless to me. So, with my four-year-old brother toddling behind me, I hurried over the next morning. Scooter watched as I pulled the sack of dry food down from the shelf and scooped some into his bowl. Just as I placed the dish on the floor, my brother reached down to pet him. Scooter lunged.

Before I could pull the panicky dog loose, my brother had sustained several bites on his chin and neck and had to go to an emergency room for stitches. Though scarred, he recovered. I never did. My fear response seemed permanently activated. Even tiny Pomeranians could reduce me to shudders with one yappy yelp.

Later, when I was six months pregnant, Bob and I bought our first house.

"This is just what we need, with a big fenced yard and all," he pronounced.

I glanced at him warily. "Remind me, why do we need a fenced yard? So that the baby can play safely?"

"And so our dog can run loose." Bob reached over and patted my hand.

"I hate dogs. They bite, they shed, they dig up flowers, and I'm scared to death of them. One bit my baby brother."

"I've always had dogs," Bob replied. "I'll find a good one."

A policeman, Bob worked swing shift. "I don't want you and the baby home alone at nights. A dog will protect you."

I hesitated. We lived in a corner house on a cul-de-sac in what appeared to be a safe suburban neighborhood. But lately, especially as Christmas drew near, Bob had been coming home at midnight with tales of residential burglaries.

"Good means not over twenty pounds," I cautioned. "And it has to be female and wooly like a poodle. I don't want hair all over the rug."

"Sounds good to me," he said, "I'll go to the pound tomorrow."

The next afternoon Bob pulled into the garage with a gargantuan German shepherd and collie mix, who bounded out of the back seat and lurched against me. As I frantically backed away I noticed several strands of hair clinging to my navy corduroy maternity smock.

"Isn't he beautiful!" Bob exclaimed.

Catching the love light shining in his eyes, I managed a weak nod. "Uh, yes, just, uh, beautiful."

He knelt beside the animal. "I'm calling him 'Christofur,' with f-u-r for his beautiful tan coat. But we can call him 'Chris' for short. He's two years old and fully housebroken."

My fingers shook as I raised my hand to point to the panting monster. "It's a he. He's huge. And I'm afraid."

"Nah," Bob said, "German shepherds and collies are good with kids. The baby will love him and so will you."

Though we put some old blankets on the floor of the utility porch, when Chris would scratch at our door at night, Bob would leap up and let the dog in.

"He can sleep at the foot of the bed," I conceded, "but not on the bed!"

Bob looked disappointed until I reminded him that the double bed barely was big enough to hold the two of us, especially with my burgeoning belly.

As Christmas neared, Chris began to dog my every step around the house. He curled up on the kitchen floor while I washed dishes. When I walked across the street to visit a neighbor, he would huddle in the bay window watching for my return. He seemed afraid to let me out of his sight.

"He's just making sure that you're okay," Bob assured me. "Dogs have a sixth sense, and he might be aware that the baby's going to be coming in another couple of months."

A few days before Christmas, Bob and I decorated our tree just before he left for work. We walked

out to the front sidewalk to admire the lights twin-
kling in the bay window.

"How about making some of those great oatmeal
cookies this evening?" Bob asked. "I'm beginning to
feel like Santa, craving cookies and milk at night."

"After I vacuum," I said.

Chris shed enough fur to stuff one of the new
king-sized mattresses I'd seen advertised on televi-
sion. So I now had to trundle around the living
room, unclogging the vacuum every few minutes,
pulling fur from the brushes and tossing it into a
paper bag.

After I took the last tray of cookies from the
oven and left them on a dish towel on the kitchen
counter to cool, I decided to run across the street for
a brief visit with a neighbor who was also expecting
a baby soon.

About an hour later, I started back to the house,
but something seemed odd. I suddenly realized that
I could see no lights in the window. When I walked
in, the first thing I saw was the Christmas tree on
its side, surrounded by shattered glass ornaments.
Chris was nowhere to be found. I walked into the
kitchen and saw that the counter was bare except for
a rumpled dish cloth and a few crumbs.

I finally found him hiding under the dining room
table, trembling. Chris just stared at me with his big

black eyes, shaking with fear. He wouldn't come out, not even when I offered him a morsel of his favorite hamburger.

When Bob came home at midnight, I had baked a fresh batch of cookies and patched up the tree the best I could, spacing out the few unbroken ornaments and stringing some popcorn to fill in the bare spots. Chris remained huddled under the table.

"I think he knocked over the tree accidentally when he went to the window to watch for me," I explained. "And then I think he gulped down the cookies, afraid that we wouldn't feed him any more."

"The people at the pound said he'd been abused," Bob said. "He's probably more afraid of you than you are of him."

"Well, let's show him that he's welcome here," I said.

Together we crawled under the table and soothed our errant pet.

On Christmas day, as I offered Chris a new red dish filled with turkey, I remembered how Scooter had attacked my brother in fear. I intended to ensure that this dog would never be afraid of me or our baby. I took a deep breath, then wrapped my arms around his neck and buried my face in his fur.

—*Terri Elders*

Adopted

"Mom! Come quick!" My nine-year-old son's voice drifted in through the kitchen window along with the fragrance of burning leaves. It was an idyllic day in late autumn. Unseasonably warm weather had beckoned my son outdoors. He knew he wouldn't have many more warm afternoons to play outside before winter arrived.

Being a mother of three, I knew not to panic and rush immediately to my son's side. Many times I have been summoned with such urgency only to find a commercial for a new, must-have toy or a ladybug crawling on the window. So I've adopted the Rule of Three: My response to the first "Hey, Mom! Come quick!" call—ignore it. To the second—"What is it?" To the third—"Okay, I'm coming."

This time, just as I expected, after a long pause my son called again, "Mom, come here!" I would have called out "What is it?" and continued cooking dinner until the third call had he not then added these words: "Can I keep him?"

Instantly, I was out the door. There, on the patio, stood the most enormous dog I had ever seen in my life. My son kneeled next to the behemoth, his arms wrapped around its massive neck, grinning from ear to ear. My knees turned to jelly and I almost fell forward. Stifling the urge to scream, I took three deep breaths. Then in a quiet monotone I said, "Get away from that dog."

"Mom, he's friendly!" cried my son. As if to prove it, this gigantic hairy mass stepped toward me wagging its tail. I thought that its tail alone must weigh ten pounds.

Now, don't get me wrong. I am an animal lover and believe with all my heart that "dogs rule." As a matter of fact, my female terrier was beside herself with joy at the prospect of a new playmate, and she was welcoming him by circling his huge body like a white, barking helicopter.

My son still had his arm around the beast's neck. I placed myself in front of the creature, hoping to shield my child in case it turned vicious. It was then that I noticed his eyes. In them, I saw a deep well of kindness. As he panted, his enormous jaws showed gleaming canine teeth, but there was no ferociousness there. In fact, if it were possible for a dog to smile, then, indeed, this dog was smiling in a goofy, lopsided way. It occurred to me that his silly grin matched the one on my son's face. I looked from boy to beast and broke into the same ridiculous grin.

"I'm naming him 'Big Boomer,'" announced my son.

In affirmation, the dog whined and stepped up to me. Shooing the revolving terrier out of the way, I extended my hand for him to sniff. He politely complied and then sat down right on my feet and leaned his enormous bulk against my legs. Shocked, I struggled to stay standing with what felt like a Mack truck parked on my feet. I reached out and patted his head. He raised his wolf-like face and looked up at me with such utter contentment that my heart melted.

I turned from my son's expectant face and looked into the big brown eyes fixed on mine. I stroked the dog's head and ran my hand down his neck. That's when I felt it; he was wearing a collar. I slid my fingers under it and gently turned it around until I was satisfied there were tags.

My son interrupted my thoughts by asking once again, "Mom, can we keep him?"

"Sweetie, this dog has on a collar. That means he belongs to someone."

"Who?"

Foolishly, I looked around like the owner was hiding behind a tree. With a mountain behind us, a cemetery on one side, and a single house on the other, where he came from was a mystery. I untangled myself from my new shaggy friend and went inside to check the newspaper, but there were no lost-dog notices. I even drove through the cemetery and asked the caretaker if he knew anything about the dog. Nothing.

Within a week, Boomer became a member of our family. Having a dog of mammoth proportions was a new experience for all of us. Grocery shopping became quite an adventure. How much do you feed a dog that size? Since it was November and the nights were cold, we tried to get him to come into the garage. He would stand and wag his tail as if to say, "Thanks, but I'm fine. I have this winter coat you see." Boomer, we had discovered, was a gentleman in every way.

Then, almost two weeks after he appeared, the phone rang early one Saturday morning. "My name is John Anderson, and I'm looking for a big yellow dog. He belongs to my mother. Someone said they thought they saw him over at your place."

Boomer had a home, and we soon discovered it was a good one. He belonged to a ninety-year-old woman who made gravy for him every morning. Her son, John, explained he had been out looking everywhere for his mother's dog. Somehow, he had traveled more than ten miles from his home to ours.

That afternoon, John came to take Boomer, who we learned they called Old Yeller. Or so he thought. Never having ridden in a vehicle before, the dog sat his immense body down on the driveway and refused to budge. No manner of treats or encouragement could cajole him into that truck. Refusing to give up, Mr. Anderson returned on Monday armed with sleeping pills from the vet. Sleeping peacefully, Boomer/Old Yeller was lifted into the truck by three strong men and driven away.

Our whole family missed Boomer. Even though he'd only been with us for a little while, we were all sad to see him go. Our two terriers, Molly and Murphy, lost the urge to run and play. My husband often remarked what a good old fellow Boomer was, and my son cried buckets of tears. I worried if Boomer had plenty to eat and a warm place to sleep.

On Thursday morning, I went downstairs to make coffee and let the dogs out. When I opened the door, there in the early morning mist stood Big Boomer! With his tail wagging and lopsided grin intact, he ran to me as if to say, "Hey Mom, I'm back!" We later discovered he had disappeared on the Monday night after he'd been returned to his owner. It had taken him from Monday to Thursday, but he'd found his way back to us. Later that morning when the phone rang, I knew it was Boomer's owner.

"Yes," I replied, "he's here."

Silence.

Before I lost my nerve, I blurted out my feelings. "Look, I don't want to take your dog, but I don't want him to get killed traveling along the highway. I promise you that if you let us have him, we will take good care of him."

Silence.

I decided to try to convince him. "I know you are good to him, but you said it was just you and your mother. Here, he has a little boy and two other dogs to play with. Maybe you could get your mother a smaller dog that would be easier for her to handle." I held my breath waiting for his reply.

"Well, I guess you're right," he said. "I'm always afraid he's going to knock her down."

In the long pause that followed, my heart started pounding. I was afraid to hope he was going to let us keep Boomer. Again I said, "I don't want to take your pet from you, but if you do decide to let us have him, he will be loved and taken good care of."

At last, Mr. Anderson said, "I know someone who has a litter of speckled pups that are going to be small dogs. I think that will be just fine with my mother. Thank you for taking in Old Yeller and looking after him."

I started to hang up the phone when I remembered I wanted to ask Mr. Anderson some questions about Boomer/Old Yeller. "Mr. Anderson, can you tell me a little about Old Yeller?"

"Well, let's see. He's had all his shots. The vet came to the house and gave them to him."

When he didn't offer any other information, I asked, "How old is he?"

"I don't know."

"You don't know? Well, what about his breed. We were wondering what his parents looked like?"

"I can't help you there. You see, he just showed up at our door one morning about a year ago. All I can tell you is he was full-grown then."

We ended our conversation with promises to keep in touch. I couldn't wait to tell everyone that Boomer was now our dog.

And that's how my family came to be adopted by Boomer. It's been more than a year now, and he seems to have put down roots with us and isn't planning to move on. Never have I known such a gentle soul in such an oversized body. His size is truly intimidating, but the biggest part of Boomer is his heart.

—Rebecca D. Elswick

Griswold the Talking Dog

I had heard of doggy geniuses, but I had never owned one until we brought home Griswold. It didn't take long for his intelligence to become apparent—although I didn't know even then that he was a talking dog. But his unusual smarts and communication skills were not what attracted me to Griswold in the first place.

What I fell in love with at the humane society was an absurd-looking mixed breed. His nose and paws were enormous, and his wiry coat went every which way. As all the other dogs barked, this goofy puppy with a face like a funny old man struggled to contain himself. Only the frantic wag of the very tip of his tail betrayed his excitement at being consid-ered for adoption. *Pick me!* it said. *Me-me-me-me-me!*

So, of course, I did.

At that first magical meeting, the only hint of his keen intellect was his eyes, so like a person's. It was one of the first things that people of quality noticed about our dog.

We never knew which breeds had combined to form such a miracle of nature. "Terrier Mix/Will Grow to 50 Pounds" read the placard on the cage at the shelter. The list of guesses grew along with his size. When he finally topped out at more than double his projected weight, the consensus seemed to rest with Irish wolfhound mix . . . mixed with what was anybody's guess.

I was a newlywed with a husband who worked nights, and although Griswold's size was intimidating enough to potential attackers that it was a comfort to me, loneliness was my greatest enemy.

Griswold was a good listener. Then, when he was still a puppy, he uttered his first "words." One day while I was washing dishes, he pointedly looked at the faucet and barked.

"If you've knocked over your water again," I scolded, "you'll just have to go get your bucket."

I turned back to the dishes, making a mental note to check on the situation when I was finished. He often knocked over his water dish, so I had taken to keeping his water in a bucket in an easily accessible basement where he could dump it to his heart's content.

A few minutes later, I heard a triumphant *clunk* behind me. There at my feet was the empty bucket. Griswold sat nearby, wagging his tail expectantly.

When I was lonely at nights, I taught Griswold tricks. It didn't take much. All I had to do was show him once or twice, and he had the trick down—as long as he got a dog cookie for his efforts. If I didn't have the cookie, he would plant himself stubbornly in place or bark at the pantry door to tell me what I had missed.

After he'd learned all of the conventional tricks, I taught him silly ones. Then I taught them in my own made-up sign language. Then I combined them into tricks like "fall down, roll over, and play dead" when I pointed my finger and said "bang." When I ran out of ideas, I finally learned that the most important trick was the one Griswold taught me: to listen to what he had to say.

And he had a lot to say. What began was the running conversation of a lifetime.

It wasn't always easy. Griswold taught me that he had his own mind. When he wanted something, he expected it because he knew I understood him. When he decided it was time for a walk, for example, he would get the leash. If I pretended I didn't understand what he wanted, he would try to force it into my hands. Who can say no to that?

One year, my sister sent Griswold a squeaky toy for Christmas. It was wrapped, so I put it under the tree with the rest of the gifts. When I passed the Christmas tree, I kept noticing that the dog's gift had the strangest tendency to roll off into the middle of the room. I put it back on the pile, sure I'd put it back before.

It wasn't until I sat down near the tree that Griswold was able to drop a bigger hint. He went straight to his beloved gift, carefully removed it from the pile, sat down, and deposited it in front of himself with a gentleness that can only be described as reverence. The paper, I noticed, wasn't crumpled in the slightest. I felt so mean when he gave me his questioning look.

"I'm sorry," I laughed, "but you'll have to wait for Christmas like the rest of us."

I resisted the urge to put it out of reach, because— I have to admit—I wanted to see what he'd do.

He did not unwrap that gift until I gave him the go-ahead and helped him with it on Christmas morning. But in the weeks before then, I did have to put it back on the pile under the tree dozens of times. And we never figured out how he knew that was his gift. It was the only one he ever touched.

When my son was born, I worried. Griswold had never been around a baby. He was the baby. How would he handle it?

The answer was that he handled it like any proud big brother, although he was a lot more generous. I had to watch him closely because he liked to give bones and dog toys to the baby.

My son's first words were very realistic-sounding barks. I will never forget the sight of my diapered baby standing next to that enormous dog at the picture window, both of them barking at squirrels. Griswold was teaching our son to be bilingual.

When my daughter was born, Griswold was entering old age. He positioned himself next to the bassinet at nap time, and when I was downstairs and heard the telltale stirrings in the baby monitor, I would also hear Griswold hoist himself up and pad down the hallway to the top of the stairs, where he would bark down to tell me our baby was awake.

As the children grew, Griswold's "vocabulary" grew to include a number of sighs and meaningful glances. When they got too wild, he would give me worried looks and bark at them to settle down.

Jumping on the beds upset him a lot. Occasionally, he would come and get me, casting worried glances in their direction as clearly as a gesture.

"Uh-oh," I'd say solemnly. "Griswold tells me you've been jumping on the furniture again."

"Does he really talk to you?" they would ask, guilty eyes round with awe.

I would explain that, although he didn't talk in words they way that we do, he knew how to communicate in many other ways, if we only paid attention. I can't count the number of times I've had to use that lesson since.

As he aged, Griswold told me when he needed help. There were times when he had to be very patient with me, but I tried hard to learn. And when the time came for Griswold to tell me that one last thing, listening was the hardest thing I'd ever had to do.

Those days are a lifetime away now—a dog's lifetime. The children are almost grown, and we've had another dog, a wonderful dog, in the interim. Our "new" dog doesn't talk the way Griswold did, but it no longer matters. Griswold taught me to listen, and that will stay with me for the rest of my life.

I've learned that all dogs communicate if we only make an effort to hear. And it isn't just dogs, either. I'm finding that the secret to dealing with any living thing—whether a pet, a plant, or a teenager—is to listen to what they aren't telling us in words.

At least, that's what Griswold the Talking Dog told me. And he was pretty smart.

—T'Mara Goodsell

Old Dog, New View

As I reached into the sudsy sink for another glass to wash, I felt a nudge on my hip. And then her whining began again. Over and over, Naya Nuki, our old mastiff, kept coming to me, pleading for attention, after I had just told her to go lay down. She would also ask for dinner with her deep *ar-oooo, ar-ooooo* five minutes after she'd finished eating, begging as if she hadn't eaten for a week. When I did give her attention or a treat, she would bounce around like a dancing circus dog, only not so gracefully, as she was not only very old, but also around 110 pounds. It was strange behavior for a dog who normally liked to lie on her bed most of the time.

Clearly, Nuki was losing her short-term memory and acting like a puppy who hadn't been trained. Once the fastest dog I'd ever trained to learn things and the slowest dog to forget anything, she now seemed to be getting senile. Even though it seemed hard to put up with, the alternative was unthinkable. After all, Nuki used to be the best dog I ever had.

When we bought her, she was the last puppy in her litter and totally attached to her mother. She whined all the way to our house. Within an hour of reaching home, though, she had bonded with each of us: me, my husband Alan, and our daughter Anna. We played with her during that hour and then ate dinner. We were amazed that she didn't beg during our meal. After the meal, Alan went to the restroom, and she followed him to the door. When he closed it, she howled, even though Anna and I called to her and finally went over to comfort her. She was inconsolable until he came out again. We were now her family, and she didn't want to let one of us out of her sight! That was when we decided to name her Naya Nuki, after the story of a Native American girl who was kidnapped by another tribe and taken more than a thousand miles away from her family, but missed them so badly that she escaped and found her way all the way home to them again.

Nuki soon learned that when people left, they would be back. Then her real training began, and what a memory that puppy had! The second day we had her, I left her in the living room while I took the laundry upstairs. When I came down, she had chewed up a pencil that she found on the floor. I caught her in the act and gave her a solid scolding, "Bad, Nuki! Don't ever chew a pencil! Bad girl!"

After that, no matter what was on the floor, she wouldn't touch it unless it was put into her bowl. A week later, Anna left several toys on the floor when we went to the store. On the way home, she remembered she'd left her precious toys with the new puppy loose in the house.

"What will I do? Those are my favorite toys!" Anna cried.

"Maybe she won't chew them up. I haven't seen her chewing anything since I scolded her for the pencil last week."

Sure enough, when we arrived home, the toys lay untouched on the floor, as did any and every other thing we put on the floor after that.

Likewise, it took only one scolding after a house-breaking accident in Anna's room for Naya Nuki to never go on the floor again.

A few months after we got her, I threw some old meat in the trash can. Nuki put her nose into the can as I was leaving the kitchen. Again, I scolded her. "No, Nuki! The garbage is not to eat!" That was ten years ago, and she had never attempted to get into the garbage again, even when I put meat scraps in it and left for several hours.

But now that her memory seemed to be slipping, I didn't know what to expect. Maybe she'd forget all the things she'd learned over the years and start getting into things. At the very least, it was exasperating to have to tell her to go lie down several times a day when she came up to beg for attention or food while I was working on something. With a sigh, I prayed for wisdom about what I should do about poor old Naya Nuki.

I contemplated how loving Nuki was, even with our tomcat, Peach Rugen. When we got him nine years ago, he claimed her spot of baby in the family for a few days. Nuki wasn't jealous, even when he smacked her face with claws out; she growled, and we yelled at her for scaring the kitten. No, she wasn't jealous, even though she became afraid to get her face near him, because he would do his kitten thing and suddenly leap up, jabbing her muzzle with his sharp little claws. She faithfully loved that feisty little kitty and would wag her tail whenever he came around. After all, he was part of her family. When Peach was grown up, if Nuki heard another tomcat in the yard yowling at him, she would go crazy trying to get out so she could chase the intruder away from her beloved brother.

Yes, Nuki was a rare dog, the likes of which I had never seen or heard of before.

Whines brought me out of my contemplation. There she was again, standing by my side and pressing her head into my hip to ask for attention. I couldn't help but pet her.

"Don't worry, Nuki, we'll figure things out."

Then the phone rang. It was my mother, who had recently moved to be near us because my father had Alzheimer's disease. She wanted to know if she could bring Dad over to my house for a couple of hours while she went to a meeting.

"Sure, Mom. It'll be good to visit with him for a while." It was hard for Mom to watch Dad constantly. He got into things, lost things, and asked her the same questions so many times that she couldn't help losing patience sometimes. So I was glad they'd moved closer so that I could help.

"Hi, Dad," I greeted him thirty minutes later. "What do you want to do? I have a newspaper you can read."

"That would be fine," he said with a grin.

Dad sat on the couch and began pulling apart the paper, searching for something interesting to read.

Naya Nuki got up from her bed and pattered over to Dad. Whining, she bumped his knee with her nose.

"Is this your dog?" he asked, even though he had seen her many times before.

"Yes, she is."

"How old is she?"

"Ten."

"Really? She's a good dog. What's her name?"

"Nuki. She loves to be petted."

I turned and saw that he was already petting her. She stood with head pressed close against his leg as he rubbed her ears. Dad kept smiling and rubbing Nuki's head and ears for a couple of minutes. Then he asked again, "How old is this dog?"

"She's ten."

"Really? She's a good dog."

For about an hour, Dad kept petting and Nuki kept leaning. He also kept asking me how old she was and saying she was a good dog.

Finally, he said, "A nap is what I need right now. Where can I lie down?"

"The couch is a recliner. You can lie on it," I said.

He leaned back, putting his feet up, and Nuki moved to his side. She leaned her head over the arm of the couch and laid her muzzle on his lap.

"How old is this dog?" Dad asked sleepily.

"She's ten."

"Really? She's a good dog."

He rubbed her ears until he fell asleep, occasionally asking me how old she was and then saying she was a good dog. When his hand slipped off her head, I thought for a minute Naya would start whining and wake him up. Instead, she walked over to her pillow and curled up on it with a contented sigh. Naya Nuki and Dad had bonded, and to her, he was now a member of her family—even better, one who forgot he'd already petted her just as she forgot she had already been petted!

Naya Nuki slept on her bed while Dad slept on the couch, both content in their view of things just as they were. "Was everything okay?" Mom asked when she came to get Dad.

"Yup. Everything went great. Dad had a good time petting Nuki, and she didn't bug me while I got my cleaning done. Bring him over more often, will you?"

Mom seemed pleased, and so was I.

Waking from his nap a few minutes later, Dad stood up and stretched. Nuki made a beeline to his side. She sensed her new family member was going somewhere, and she wanted some loving first.

"Oh, a dog!" he said with surprise. "How old is this dog?"

"She's ten, Dad."

"She's a good dog," he said, smiling as he patted her head goodbye.

Yes, Nuki was a good old dog. In fact, she was still the best dog I've ever had.

—*Suzanne Endres*

I.Q. Test

We woke that morning to a chorus of puppy laughter—or so we thought—and tried to imagine what our rascals were up to. Running? Jumping? Pummeling each other? Had they invented a new game with their favorite tennis ball?

We had arrived at the decision to have pups by a circuitous route, and there would be only one litter. For our son and daughter, it would be a once-in-a-lifetime opportunity to observe birth and, sadly, death and to experience the joys, heartbreaks, and responsibilities of helping to raise a family of lively canines. We hoped that the experience would help our children to develop a deep respect for these creatures that so many still refer to as "dumb animals."

With the birth of the puppies, the dogs far outnumbered the people in our family. Our pack included not only the pups and their mother (a husky-malamute mix) but also their father (shepherd-rottweiler) and honorary grandmother (yellow Lab). We all enjoyed the privilege of watching firsthand the workings of a dog family: the hierarchy, the training and disciplining of the pups, the gentleness and affection they showed to one another.

Most nights the pups slept in the kitchen, in the same large plywood box where they had been born, and in the morning we would trip over each other trying to be the first into the room to see their seven heads simultaneously pop up over the side of the box to greet us. But since the weather had been so balmy the previous night, we had let them sleep outside in the dog run. Now, there was so much excitement in their yips and yaps that we decided not to interrupt, for a while, at least. The pups were seven and a half weeks old, and five of them would soon leave us for new homes and new lives. We would not have many more such opportunities to enjoy their puppy play, so we lay back and enjoyed the sounds of their romping.

After about ten minutes with no change in the activity level, I decided it was time to check on them. I went to my son's bedroom to look out at the dog run, a large fenced-in area with lawn and dirt and lots of room to run and play. What I found was not at all what I expected. At the far end of the run was a nonfunctioning hot tub, and a half circle of pups were gathered at the side of it, jumping in place like cheerleaders, shouting encouragement to the pup in the center, who was digging wildly just at the edge of the tub. An escape route? Trying to find China? Though I knew that at some point they would have to learn not to dig up the yard, I didn't have the heart to start that lesson just yet. I stood at the door and watched as the digging and cheering continued.

Finally, after another five minutes or so, I walked out for a closer look; when I saw what was really happening, I froze. Until that moment, I had not bothered to count the number of pups in the circle. I had assumed it was six, but it was only five. Five pups in the cheering circle. One in the middle digging. And the seventh peering out from beneath the hot tub. How he had gotten there, I could not imagine. There was no weight on him. He was not in any pain or danger. He just could not get out. Though the puppies seemed so sure of themselves, the task seemed impossible. Staring at them as they continued digging and cheering, I puzzled over what to do. The only solution I could think of was to lift the hot tub. But, even though it was empty and I was pretty strong for my size, I could not lift it myself.

I did the only thing I could in that situation. "Jason, go get your father," I called to my eleven-year-old son. "Hurry!"

I knew my husband would either be able to lift the tub or to find another way to rescue the puppy. So, while my son went to fetch Superman, I waited and watched and wrung my hands.

The pup doing the digging was Bruskyjack. He had been the last born of the seven and had gotten off to a precarious start. Their mother, after having given birth to so many, had been tired and not immediately able to care for him as she had the previous six. Without proper stimulation, he would not start breathing. My husband had wrapped him in a towel, and then he and I took turns holding the puppy, keeping him warm and rubbing him to encourage respiration. When we were sure he was out of danger, we put him back with his mother and the rest of the litter. Our reward was a big, sweet pup whose favorite activity was eating and who most observers labeled as being not too bright. On that day in early July, Bruskyjack proved them wrong.

While I watched, the digging stopped, and Bruskyjack, along with the circle of cheerleaders, backed away quietly. That was when I turned my attention to the pups' mother. Through all of this commotion, she had been lying to the side with her head on her paws, watching, waiting, and thinking—wisely allowing her son to do his job. As soon as the pups were out of the way, she stood up, walked to the hot tub, pushed her snout into the hole Brusky had dug, and pulled free her wayward pup.

By the time my husband arrived, the problem had been solved and tragedy averted. The rescued pup was receiving a motherly spit-bath, the others were quiet, and Bruskyjack was the hero of the day.

Many tests have been devised to determine a dog's intelligence. One is to put a blanket or towel over the dog's head and see how long it takes for him to get out. Of course, the faster, the smarter. We tried this with Brusky when he was a few years old. After turning around a few times and carefully evaluating the situation, he decided to lie down and take a nap. But, as J.C. Hare and A.W. Hare wrote, "Heroism is active genius." And by that measure, Bruskyjack was truly a dog genius.

—*Mary Rudy*

Since I Fell for Chuck

Being a mom of adult children can be difficult, but being a mom to my daughter's boyfriend and his dog was not what I signed up for. Nevertheless, I told my twenty-two-year-old daughter, Annie, that her boyfriend, Tim, could stay for a while until he found a place to live. And, of course, his adorable chocolate Lab puppy, Chuck, could stay too, but only if he wouldn't chase my three cats.

Over the months, I grew fond of Tim, who helped me fix things around the house. We eventually made a deal: he'd be my handyman in exchange for rent. As a single mom, I thought it was a dream come true and immediately began making lists of things to be repaired: the broken bathroom fan, the light socket in the dining room chandelier, the hinge on the cat door . . .

After a while, though, the jobs became less home-related and more dog-related. My newly sown lawn was Chuck's first target; he'd dig a new hole every day. Tim tried everything to divert him—dog treats to dog toys—but nothing worked.

I was exasperated. Now, I was paying Tim to fix things around the house and to clean up the messes that his dog made.

One day I got a message at work: "You need to get your dog out of my backyard!" Chuck had broken through the gate into the yard next door, and my neighbor was annoyed.

I quickly called her back. "What happened?"

"Chuck pinned my daughter against the house and tried to jump up on her."

I smiled to myself, figuring that he was probably just trying to give her a kiss. "Oh, he's just a puppy," I explained. "He won't hurt her—"

"I don't care," she interrupted. "My daughter's afraid of dogs, and he scared her."

I wanted to say, "But she's nineteen. Can't she see he's just a puppy?" Instead, I managed to say, "I'm sorry, I'll handle this."

Then I called my daughter at work and asked her to find Tim.

Within fifteen minutes, Tim arrived to the rescue and found Chuck running circles around my neighbor and her daughter, who were then cowered in a corner of their yard.

That night I called a meeting with Annie and Tim. "This dog has got to go," I announced. "First, he digs holes in my lawn, and now he terrorizes the neighbors."

"Oh, give me a break," Annie protested. "He wasn't 'terrorizing' them."

"And just the other day," I continued, "someone broke my windshield wiper and left another note threatening to call the police if Chuck keeps barking."

"Who did that?" Tim demanded to know.

"I don't know and I don't care. I'm done."

The room was quiet. Chuck brought his duck toy over to Tim and nuzzled him to play catch. "Not now, boy." Annie interceded. "Mom, Tim offered to build a fence so Chuck stays in our yard."

I looked at Tim. "What kind of a fence?"

"Well, I've been thinking, I can fence off part of the yard for Chuck and keep him off the new lawn at the same time. He doesn't need that much room."

I couldn't believe I was even thinking about a fence, much less keeping this dog. I looked over at Chuck, who had now dragged his duck toy over to the corner of the room, where he was playing happily by himself.

"Let me think about this."

I spent the next few days agonizing over what to do. Chuck couldn't leave without Tim, and that would make Annie unhappy. Besides, I had to admit, I'd miss Chuck, who now charged into my room every morning and woke me up with wet, sloppy kisses.

It was after one of those wake-up kisses that I decided to at least try Tim's fence idea before booting Chuck. I gave myself a deadline—four weeks after the fence was up.

A few days later, I met Tim after work at Home Depot. He picked out the fencing material—and, of course, I paid for it.

"Your fence doesn't give Chuck enough room," I said when I took a good look at Tim's plans. "What if we let him have the run of the old vegetable garden too? I haven't prepared it yet this year."

"Are you sure?" Tim was surprised.

"He's got to be able to run during the day, right? None of us is home to walk him." I felt foolish. What do I know about dogs? I'm a cat person!

"It's your call, Marilee."

First, my lawn; now, my vegetable garden. I felt like I was losing my mind. One day I was throwing Chuck's duck toy for him; the next I was complaining he's too much work, there's dog hair everywhere, and he's scaring the cats.

Once the fence was finished, we got into a routine. Tim resumed his household chores, Chuck ran around in his new play area, and the neighbors stopped complaining. At night we'd sometimes sit around the living room playing with Chuck. I even got good at throwing his duck toy so he could catch it on the fly.

Forget the rule about not throwing stuff in the living room.

Forget the deadline.

Every morning, I'd still ask who was going to walk Chuck. Annie and Tim always promised to do it later. After they left for work, Chuck would nuzzle up to me at the kitchen table, where I'd be trying to finish my coffee and read the paper. Eventually, I'd look into his big, brown Lab eyes and dissolve.

"Okay, Chuck, let's go. I'll take you."

Then I'd get up, grab the leash and a few plastic doggie bags, and off we'd go.

After a while, I finally stopped asking who was going to walk Chuck and just made it part of my morning routine. Chuck and I would take a different route from day to day, so I got to see gardens I'd never seen before and meet neighbors I didn't know.

"Your garden is one of my favorites," I greeted one of my neighbors who lived two doors down from me and was busy planting.

"Thank you."

"Chuck!" I yanked him away from her new plants. "Sorry, he's just a puppy."

"It's okay. He's a sweet dog. What kind is he?" She bent down to pet Chuck, who immediately started licking her hand.

"He's a Lab," I said just as Chuck pulled me toward the next house. "Gotta go!" I called over my shoulder as we headed down the street together.

"You need to be trained," I said to Chuck in my most authoritative voice.

Chuck wasn't listening. I tried to remember what I'd learned in that dog-training class I'd taken a while back. I'd asked Tim once if I could take Chuck for training, but he disapproved. Chuck already had enough training, he told me, but he thought I could use some. So I paid for a couple of classes, and Chuck and I attended. He ate all the treats and learned nothing. I was instructed to let my dog know I was in charge. So much for dog training!

Chuck lunged toward another garden, pulling me in tow. I peeked through the gate and saw a beautiful, brown shingled house sitting amidst redwoods, ferns, and rhododendrons.

"Chuck, check this out!" I whispered to him. "This house was probably built around 1900."

Chuck looked at me and then tried to jump up and lick me.

"Down!" I laughed pushing him away. "Come on, it's time to go home. I've got to get to work." I glanced at my watch and reached for my cell phone, forgetting for the moment that I'd left it at home. I had decided early on that I didn't want to bring it on these walks. No work allowed, just time alone for me and Chuck.

One morning I woke up sick. This time, not even Chuck's big brown eyes could persuade me to take a walk. Looking him straight in the face, I said firmly, "No walks today, Chuck. I'm going to bed." I was barely back under the sheets when he landed, all forty pounds, at my side. I slept most of the day, awakening only to Chuck's snores and a few wet kisses on my cheeks.

On weekends, I'd sometimes take Chuck on a run in the hills behind my house. We both needed the exercise. He'd race back and forth, coaxing me to run and play with him. I did my best to keep up, but eventually I'd have to say, "Sorry, Chuck, it's time to go." I'd put his leash back on him, and we'd stagger back to the car, where I'd get my water bottle and pour some into a bowl for Chuck. I drank the rest.

One evening, I was reading on the couch with Chuck lying across my feet when Tim walked in cradling my favorite cat, Oscar, in his arms. Tim and I looked at each other, Chuck and Oscar looked at each other, and in that moment I knew we had become family: one dog, three cats, my daughter, her boyfriend, and me.

And we were a family . . . until one day, a year and a half later, Annie announced that she and Tim were breaking up. He and Chuck would be moving out.

"What do you mean, breaking up?" I was aghast. "I thought everything had settled down around here."

"Maybe for you, Mom."

Over the months, I had been so focused on my relationship with Chuck that I hadn't paid much attention to Annie and Tim's relationship. As the departure day approached, I couldn't keep it in anymore. "I don't want to interfere, but I just have to ask, can Chuck visit sometimes?"

Annie shot me a look that clearly said "No."

Tim said, "Sure."

But I knew that Chuck wouldn't be visiting any time soon, if ever. It's not fair that adult children only have to ask if their friends and animals can move into my house but that they don't have to ask if they can move out. No matter what I told myself, though, nothing could change the fact that Chuck was leaving. And I was devastated.

The house became quiet again. Now, when I returned home, no dog rushed to greet me while the cats scattered to get out of his way. I tried returning to the fire trail where Chuck and I had run together, but it was too lonely without him. Instead, I walked in the neighborhood, but I didn't usually get too far before returning home in tears.

A few months passed. One afternoon, Annie and I were looking through the mail together.

"Hey, what's this?" Annie held up an envelope with dog and cat faces on it. "It's from Pet Adoptions."

No secrets in this house, I thought to myself. "They had a table outside the produce market, so I signed their mailing list," I explained. "I thought I might volunteer."

Annie didn't buy it. "Come on, Mom, admit it," she teased, "you know you want a dog."

My cover was blown.

"You know, I really fell for that Chuck," I confessed. "He didn't just move into my house, he moved into my heart."

Now, I was ready for the real deal—a dog of my own.

—*Marilee Stark*

No Job Training Required

I've often considered how each creature of nature is so exquisitely fitted to its niche. Fish balance their bodies in a current with the slightest adjustments in their fins. Hawks spread a few wing feathers to steer their way through the updrafts of thermals and then reconfigure their aerodynamics for a dive when they spot potential food.

Dogs, however, are the animals I marvel at most, perhaps because they are so close in my daily life and easy to observe at all times. I resist doing them the disservice of thinking of them as people in fur suits, although they may regard me as some sort of naked and not-too-savvy dog.

I wish I had their sense of smell, of hearing, and the uncanny ability to read each other's intentions by detecting the subtlest of body movements, tail positions, ear twitches, and eye contact. They are living lie detectors. It is their means of survival in the hierarchy of the pack. And their ability to pick up the slightest nuance of body and facial language or tone of voice makes them master manipulators of the unwary human. Anyone lucky enough to have a truly close relationship with a dog and to be accepted into the pack consisting of dog and human knows he (or she) must be the alpha wolf, so to speak. Humans can control resources such as food, water, and comfortable places to sleep. Dogs can use their innately superior senses to try to gain the upper hand. Dogs can read humans much better than the other way around.

I was always aware of these behaviors and instincts, but never so acutely as on one unforgettable summer night.

L'anse and Bonavista, my pair of four-year-old champion Newfoundlands, had traveled thousands of miles, seen thousands of people and been petted by hundreds. They'd had close contact with people of all manner of dress and disposition. To my knowledge, they had never met anyone they didn't tolerate. Adaptable to almost anything due to their show careers, they rested comfortably in motels with no problem and the car was like a second home. Bank tellers sent treats out with the deposit slips in the drive-in lane. Tail-wagging enthusiasm greeted gas station attendants at the expectation of pats and dog biscuits proffered through open windows.

As a breed, Newfoundlands are known for their soft facial expressions and sweet, accepting nature. Their long, thick, black coats invite hugging, and the slowly waving tails assure admirers of their benign temperament. Some people mistakenly couple the large size, deliberate movement, and laid-back nature for slow wit, but I knew how intelligent and intuitive this magnificent breed could be.

These traits were exhibited in a way I had never before witnessed when I chose these two as my traveling companions and set out on a long trip.

I planned to drive from New Mexico to New Jersey with several stops, but the first day on the road merged into an evening that was cooler than expected for July. So I decided to keep on driving through the night and check into an air-conditioned motel to sleep with the Newfs during the heat of the day. Well after midnight on the first leg of our journey, I stopped at a coffee shop in Amarillo, Texas. I rolled all the windows in the station wagon down halfway. The "girls" would be cool but would not jump out. They were so used to traveling that they knew the rules very well.

In the restaurant, I took a seat in a booth. Two young men occupied a nearby table. We were the only customers in the room. After serving my coffee, the sole waitress resumed reading her magazine.

"Hey," one man called over to me. "Where you from?"

I held my coffee mug in both hands and pretended to read the dessert menu that was propped between the salt and pepper shakers.

"Are you traveling alone?" the other asked.

I didn't want to be unfriendly, but something about this situation unnerved me. If I spoke, would that send a signal that I was interested in further conversation? If I ignored them, would they be more persistent?

"Not really," I answered their question. It was the truth. Perhaps they would think my husband was in the car taking a nap.

"Where are you headed?"

Maybe they were locals and just curious about a stranger at that hour of the night. "To my brother's house," I said, hoping they wouldn't detect what I truly inept liar I was.

"Why don't you come on over here and sit with us? We don't bite."

"No, thanks. I need to get going as soon as I finish my coffee."

The pair got up, threw some money on the table, and left. When my cup was empty, I refused a refill but waited a few minutes more before going back to my car.

I had a grip on the driver's door handle when an arm extended over my right shoulder. The hand at the end of the arm pressed against the top of the driver's door, holding it closed. Fingers had a firm grasp of my left shoulder. Was one man behind me or two? I couldn't tell.

A pitiful few options for action flashed through my mind. My heart raced. I was so frozen with fright that I couldn't even scream.

Two black heads were already straining out of the open window of the rear door. Bonnie and L'anse, their lips drawn back, showed rows of white teeth gleaming in the neon light as menacing, deep-throated growls, increasing in volume, filled the night.

In retrospect, I am amazed that two human beings could move as fast as those two men did. Across the parking area they sprinted—shoving and grabbing at each other in a mad scramble to get into their pickup truck. Exhaust fumes and smoking hot rubber from squealing tires polluted the clear air.

I collapsed in my driver's seat, trembling from fear and relief combined, and waited until I was sure the truck wasn't coming back. No headlights other than mine broke the darkness of the highway nor did any appear behind me when I pulled back onto old Route 66.

L'anse and Bonnie again relaxed in the back of the wagon. They could easily have broken the window and pursued the men, but they had done what they needed to do and no more.

They read the situation and acted accordingly. I have no doubt they would have done whatever was necessary had the circumstances dictated a different course.

What had triggered the Newfs behavior? Did the scent of my adrenaline surge cue them? Was it my body language or that of the threatening men? There is no way to know for certain, only conjecture on the part of animal behaviorists. But I believe my Newfs used all their special senses to read the cues that night.

I never again heard that deep growl or saw those formidable teeth bared in a snarl. Bonnie and L'anse were as friendly as ever when men approached my car, and their attitude toward all people was as amiable as it had been prior to the incident that night. But my new awareness of their primal instincts has prompted me to pack a Newfoundland whenever I'm hitting the road.

—*Ann E. Vitale*

Girl's Best Friend

Seeing the birth of nine puppies is more educational than anything learned in a fourth-grade classroom. So I'm glad it worked out that I was home from school the day our dog had her puppies. Multiplication tables would be there tomorrow: The chance to see a new life beginning wouldn't.

What a difference a week makes. Just seven days prior, my parents were disagreeing with a friend who insisted that Brie, our Airedale terrier, was pregnant.

"She's not pregnant, she's just furry," my mom said, which was true. While show-dog Airedales are clipped year-round, pet Airedales living in Pittsburgh are kept warm and wooly during the winter months, at least in our house.

To be safe, though, Mom took Brie to the vet the next day and received the unexpected news.

"Any day now," the vet confirmed, after feeling her round belly.

Brie had a habit of slipping out through the fence at night and apparently had encountered a friendly suitor during one of her midnight romps about nine weeks prior.

Three days later, as I was tinkering on the piano, my mom yelled from the basement, "It's time!" I raced downstairs to see Brie lying on her side and a small, wet, four-legged ball slide out from behind her. Over the next few hours, eight more followed.

Our older dog, Mike, had no idea how to respond to the squirmy, squiggly creatures crawling and whimpering about. But Brie did. With us, she was a reserved dog. With her puppies, however, she was very nurturing, instinctively knowing exactly what their needs were and how to meet them. My sister and I were in our glory. Nine puppies to hold, pet, and play with. I kissed, cuddled, and snuggled all of them, but one pup in particular grabbed ahold of my heart: the four-legged ball that had arrived first that morning.

He sure is a tubbo, I thought to myself, watching him push, shove, and grunt his way past his siblings in search of food from his mother. It may not have been a word, but it was the only way for a nine-year-old to describe him. He was fatter and rounder than his brothers and sisters. Before long, the invented word became his name: Tubbo. And as he grew, he grew on me.

In the middle of the night, I'd snatch Tubbo from the pen my dad had made and sneak him to my room. Once or twice I fell asleep with him next to me, only to wake to whimpering cries, because he had wedged his plump behind between the bed and floor.

Tubbo was a typical puppy: a curious, mischievous bundle of energy. His siblings performed comic skits of their own, but this chubby pup and I made an instant connection. When the puppies were old enough, the search for permanent homes began. Friends were contacted, newspaper ads were placed, and one by one each puppy left our house to start their new lives. Within a few weeks, two puppies remained: Tubbo and his only remaining sibling, a sister. And one day a couple stopped by, looking to adopt a male dog. And my dad looked at Tubbo. And a little girl fled to her room in tears.

I don't recall my parents specifically saying we weren't keeping any puppies. Perhaps it was just understood. But to a child, if it's not talked about, maybe it's not real. Santa Claus is real until your parents tell you he isn't. Two strangers standing in your basement ready to take your dog is very real.

I lay in my bed forever, face in the pillow, listening to the three of them talking. Listening to the couple's car drive away brought a fresh wave of sadness. Listening to my dad's footsteps approaching and my bedroom door opening. I couldn't look at him. I didn't want to hear the "Now, Kelli, you knew we weren't going to keep him" speech that would just make me feel worse.

I felt a wet nose, heard a soft whimper, smelled puppy breath, and peeked from my pillow to see Tubbo trying to chew my hair.

"What happened?" I asked incredulously, as I scooped up the bundle of puppy-nipping fur.

"I told the guy, 'I'm sorry, I can't give you this dog. He belongs to my daughter,'" Dad said. And then he left my room.

My dad isn't one for displays of affection. Giving a hug and a kiss is okay; showering with love is embarrassing. He shows his love through actions: giving gifts, helping someone move furniture, mowing the lawn . . . getting his daughter's puppy back.

Tubbo grew into an eighty-pound Airedale mix (we never did find out who the father was). Discipline was not his strongest trait; loyalty was. Although he was loyal and gentle with everyone in our family, he was truly my best friend. The same pillow I cried into the day I thought I'd lost him consumed many tears as I grew up—tears over boyfriends, failed school exams, family struggles, and everyday life.

My bedroom door squeaked, so anyone trying to enter couldn't do so unannounced. Like any teenager,

I relished my privacy, especially during the mood swings and frustrations that every adolescent experiences. "Leave me alone!" I'd shout to the sound of approaching footsteps and the door creaking open. But the *tap-tap-tap* of toenails on hardwood, a snout bursting through the door, and a tail swishing against the wall received a different response. I'd open my eyes to see my four-legged pal standing at the foot of the bed. "How can I help?" he seemed to be asking.

After my college graduation, I lived at home for the summer and planned to move to Washington, D.C., in the fall. I was all grown up and ready to spread my wings. I think Tubbo, who was thirteen years old, felt his time to leave had arrived too. We had shared long talks and long walks, but things were changing and I was moving on. A few weeks before I left home forever, Tubbo passed away. His ashes are buried in my parents' backyard, under the bush that was his favorite resting spot on a hot summer day.

I've moved and unpacked boxes in many cities since, but I never have to look too deep in my keepsakes to find a picture of my best friend. I watched him enter this world and kissed him goodbye when he left. If that experience doesn't create a connection, nothing will.

—*Kelli L. Robinson*

The Convert

I now understand dog lovers. It has taken a number of years and an assortment of animals, but I am now a bona fide member of the canine fan club. And the credit goes to Buffy, who entered my life six years ago at a low point in a generally pleasant life.

I had recently retired from a prep school where I had taught for eighteen years, and though necessary, the parting from a career I loved was nonetheless a painful one. Our three sons were on their own, leading interesting lives in faraway places. My husband was still living a nine-to-five life. So, in the daytime, it was an empty-feeling house. I needed a buddy.

Why I thought "dog" in response to that need is surprising. Though there had been a series of animals in my life, the track record wasn't a good one. Our marriage began with Shark, Whale, and Tuna—three goldfish that soon became floaters.

Then there was Dublin, our first dog. He was a beautiful Irish setter with an I.Q. of seven. He could spot rabbits at a good distance but failed to observe the children in that line-of-sight path. It really wasn't that bad. Our boys were three and four and close to the ground anyway. Dublin was eventually returned to a farm, where his lack of intellectual prowess was not a problem. There were several kittens that sadly never became cats. In general, desert life in Carefree, Arizona, was not a safe home for them. Then there was Gretchen, our dachshund. Sadly, when you are a short, fat female with facial hair, you don't get a lot of respect. Short and fat was followed by a beauty with blue eyes. Portia, a rescued Alaskan malamute, was my son Colin's good deed. But her history got the best of her, and with one swift bite, she got the best of his new kitten, Jingle Bells. So we lost two animals that day; both victim and predator no longer lived in our happy home.

Despite the troubled history, I concluded that a dog was what I needed at this point in my life. And so the pursuit began.

The search for said dog was not really a positive experience either. I was interviewed at the ABC animal shelter in north Phoenix. I had fallen hard for this cute little poodle mix. To be rejected as an owner for an abandoned dog was hard to take in my less-than-ideal emotional state. With effort, I convinced myself that I really was a worthy person, and two weeks later I responded to a "moving and can't take dog" ad. I clicked with this dog too—a cute little bichon. She was licking my face and treating me like her long-lost friend. The owner angrily accused me of hiding treats in my pocket and decided to take her dog with her to Pennsylvania. It was probably a good thing. The owner seemed needier than I.

It was our housekeeper, Mary Jane (a serious dog lover), who came to my aid. She knew of an older couple who had two dogs, and the finances required for their care was becoming a problem. That is how we met Buffy.

She was an older dog of undetermined origin (a "poodle-something") and weighed about ten pounds. (This was good, because small bowel movements were something I was hoping for.) She was cute and had a great smile. From the very beginning, it was as if we were somehow joined at the hip. She would follow me from room to room and jump into my lap once I was seated. Buff was great at giving and receiving affection. My husband was a German shepherd kind of person, and Buffy is definitely a frou-frou dog, but in a matter of days, even he was wrapped around her little paw.

Buffy has been a part of our family for six years.

We began our time together as middle-aged women. She has aged at a faster pace and is now about ninety on her calendar. She is missing about half of her teeth, and her hearing is not too good. She no longer jumps into our laps. That is okay. We are growing old together. When I am ninety, I doubt that I will jump into anyone's lap either. With Buffy, I have previews of coming attractions. And I think I understand God a little better too—the whole unconditional love thing. I am still working on loving that way. Maybe, with Buffy's mentoring, by the time I'm her age, I'll be good at it too.

She has truly been a gift. So now I get it: Dogs on the family Christmas card. Dogs with jeweled collars. Thousand–dollar vet bills. Dogs on vacation. Doggie barkeries. Dogs riding shotgun on a trip to the bank. Dogs in the bed. Thanks to Buffy, I now understand it all.

—Maryann McCullough

To Mugs, With Love

Mugs never really belonged to anybody, but I don't think she knew that. Community Dog of Hickory Springs was a role she took seriously. Before my husband Dick and I ever saw the place, Mugs had wandered into the development and made it her home.

She treated all of us who owned the ten cabins nestled about our small, spring-fed lake in East Texas as her people. She came wiggling out to meet us when we first arrived, and she ran to greet us each time we drove through the gate thereafter. Mugs was love with a tail wagging behind. When she was happy, Mugs smiled. Unfortunately, a couple of crooked front teeth caused the foolish grin that inspired her name. Her sleek black body always glistened; if she got dirty, she headed to the lake and frolicked in the water.

When the full-time dogs of cabin owners came along to the lake, Mugs played with them, behaving like a gracious hostess. She seemed to understand that their rules and status differed from her own. Mugs never tried to follow them into the comfort of their homes when the day's romp ended and lights began to appear in the cabins.

On cold or stormy nights, we invited Mugs inside, where she settled onto a spot beside the fireplace, barely moving until morning. She relished those rare indulgences but never tried to claim them as her right. Mugs' life was outdoors and she knew it.

Most of us came to the lake only on weekends and holidays. However, a couple families lived there, and they looked out for Mugs while the rest of us worked in the city. My husband and I took her to town for shots, which she endured bravely, though with reproachful glances. We saw to it that she had heartworm pills.

Everyone saved Mugs a few bites at dinner, and some of us filled bowls with dry dog food too. She never begged, but she showed up each evening and accepted what food we offered, with a lick for the hand that fed her.

Everyone in our little community could always count on Mugs to amble along beside us for a walk in the piney woods around the lake. When we went fishing, her eyes never left the water. If somebody cried, "I caught one!" she would dance in a circle, as delighted as we, and then watch while the fish was released and swam away. If she considered this a peculiar ritual, she never let on.

Mugs adored the children who sometimes visited. They draped themselves around her neck, and she played with them until they were all exhausted. Then she'd flop down with that ridiculous grin spread across her face and fall asleep, wherever she might be.

Though friendly, Mugs was no coward. She once stood her ground between a snake and me, snarling until it slithered away. She never filled the role of watchdog because she accepted everyone. Strangers were just new friends. Only once did someone betray her trust . . .

When we arrived that Friday evening, Mugs led us to her litter of puppies, appearing eager for us to share this exciting event. Her babies had been born under our house, a distinct honor.

Mugs was a concerned and loving mother. She brought me the smallest puppy, carrying it tenderly in her mouth, and deposited it at my feet with a soft whine. I took over for a couple of days, feeding the tiny one milk with an eyedropper and keeping the pup warm until it was strong enough to hold its own with the others. Mugs' look when I returned it to her side was an eloquent thank you.

We spread the word that, as soon as the puppies were older, we'd take them to town and find families for them. We thought that would be easy, because Mugs had produced a cuddly, inquisitive group of three boys and three girls. What joy they would bring to their adoptive families, and how they would love being someone's best pal.

We returned a couple weeks later to discover the puppies gone and Mugs wandering frantically from house to house, searching for them. Our neighbor cried as she told us that a man from the far end of the lake had waited until Mugs was away from her babies, then piled them into a sack and killed them. She was afraid to try to stop him. None of the rest of us spoke to the man afterward, and eventually he moved away.

Soon after the puppies died, we had Mugs spayed, regretting only that we hadn't acted sooner. We thought of taking her home with us, but we already had two dogs and one more seemed one too many. Her other friends at the lake discussed finding a family for Mugs. That seemed like a good idea at first, but the more we considered it, the less certain we became. Mugs already had a home and people she considered her family. No one wanted her to move away, and would she really be happier if we took her from those she loved and the woods she knew? In the end, we did nothing. How I wish we could change that decision.

One sunny Saturday morning we arrived at the lake and, for the first time I could remember, Mugs didn't come bounding out, barking joyously. We wasted no time finding someone who could tell us where she was. I think I already knew. No one could ever convince her to stay away from the dangerous stretch of highway passing our small, quiet community between Livingston and Woodville, Texas.

When I drive into Hickory Springs, I always feel I have come home. But my heart will never lift in quite the same way at the gate. Mugs is gone. She seemed at ease with the life fate dealt her and lived it to the fullest. She loved generously, and those who knew Mugs always smile when her name is mentioned. Not a bad epitaph for a little stray dog.

—*Ramona John*

Contributors

Lynne S. Albers ("Sometimes You Limp") is the proud mom of Jennifer and Wade and a former elementary school teacher who now relaxes in the New Mexico sunshine with her husband Bob and their beagle Phoebe. She teaches coping skills to children of alcoholic/addicted parents at D.R.E.A.M summer camps and volunteers on behalf of the environment.

Teresa Ambord ("Sheriff Bean and His Posse" and "Smart Girl") lives in Northern California with her small posse of dogs. She is a business writer, freelance writer, and foster mom for dogs who need a soft place to fall. She encourages dog lovers to visit Another Chance Animal Welfare League online (ACAWL.org) to find a new furry best friend.

Suzanne Baginskie ("Dog Most Wanted") has worked for twenty-eight years as a paralegal. Originally from New Jersey, she moved to the west coast of Florida in 1970. Suzanne loves to inspire other writers and teaches creative writing at a local college. She's published numerous fiction and nonfiction short stories in anthologies and magazines.

Karen Louise Baker ("That Sheppi Smile") lives in Napa Valley, California, with her husband and their two dogs, seven cats, two horses, flock of sheep, and herd of cattle. She works with her husband, a veterinarian. She is a past recipient of the Jessamyn West Writing Award and is published in a Jessamyn West anthology of literary contest winners.

Jeanne Bogino ("Nobody Beats the Wiz") writes in western Massachusetts, where she lives with her partner, two Labrador mixes, and two gerbils named Marjorine and Mr. Slave. She has published horror, fantasy, romance, and gay fiction. By day, she is the director of a small but busy library in rural New York.

Lori Bottoms ("Bear's Boys") has published articles in magazines and news journals and essays in several anthologies, including *A Cup of Comfort® for Mothers and Sons*. She divides her time between working on her third novel, singing with an award-winning Sweet Adeline chorus, and spending time with her six grandchildren. Lori lives in Oklahoma with her two dachshunds, Seemore Bottoms and Rock Bottoms.

Elizabeth Brewster ("Miss Stinky: Queen for a Day" and "Taming the Beast") lives with her husband, Damon, two cats, and her dog, Tuck in Portland, Oregon. She and Tuck spend every spare moment hiking the beautiful mountains of Oregon. When not hiking, Elizabeth teaches and writes and Tuck chews up the furniture.

Jenn Brisendine ("Big as Life") lives in western Pennsylvania with her husband and two sons. After thirteen years of teaching secondary English, she now writes educational materials and pursues fiction and nonfiction projects. Her creative nonfiction is represented in the anthology *The Maternal Is Political* (Seal Press, May 2008) and in the online magazine *Literary Mama*.

Leslie Budewitz ("Blackie's Gift") is a writer and lawyer who lives with her husband near Bigfork, Montana, at the foot of the Swan Range. She gardens, reads, cooks, hikes in the wilderness, and draws and paints. Blackie and his gang are gone now, but his humans are readying themselves for a new dog and cat.

Kathe Campbell ("No Bones about It") lives on a Montana mountain with her mammoth donkeys, a keeshond, and a few kitties. She is a prolific writer on Alzheimer's, and her stories are found in numerous anthologies, e-zines, and medical journals.

Kay Cavanaugh ("A Boy and His Dog") is a retired nurse educator who does volunteer work with senior citizen groups. She writes for a hobby and has been published in many journals and anthologies, including other *Cup of Comfort®* books. Kay lives in Powder Springs, Georgia, with her two miniature schnauzers, Maggie and Lexie.

Loy Michael Cerf ("Gramps and the Harem") is an animal-loving, Chicago-area freelance writer. She enjoys crocheting blankets for Project Linus and dreaming up creative ways to coerce her grown children into pet-sitting, so she can guiltlessly cruise the globe with her husband of thirty-something years.

Talia Carner ("Not a Dog Lover"), a novelist and formerly the publisher of *Woman* magazine and a lecturer at international women's economic forums, resides in New York City. Her heart-wrenching suspense novels, *Puppet Child* and *China Doll*, have garnered rave reviews and are often the choice of reading groups in the United States and abroad. Her addictions include chocolate, ballet, hats, and social justice.

Terri Elders ("Christofur's Christmas") lives near Colville, Washington, with her husband, Ken Wilson. Her stories have appeared in periodicals and anthologies. In 2006, she received the UCLA Alumni Community Service Award for her work with Peace Corps and VISTA. She is a licensed clinical social worker (LCSW) and a public member of the Washington State Medical Commission.

Rebecca D. Elswick ("Adopted") teaches advanced placement English, photojournalism, and creative writing at Grundy High School. She lives with her husband, son, and four dogs in Grundy, Virginia. Her twins are currently attending college. Her fiction has appeared in the *Literary Journal of the Virginia Writing Project*, the *Jimnson Weed*, *Bewildering Stories*, and *Christmas Blooms*.

Suzanne Endres ("Old Dog, New View") has a pug, a boxer, and a mastiff-mix (Naya Nuki) as well as other pets. She writes feature articles for the "In a Pug's Eye" column of *PugTalk Magazine*. Suzanne loves to hang out with her grandkids, play with her pets, raise gardens, and write. She lives in Washington State.

Melissa Face ("Old Dog Smell") lives with her husband Craig and their beloved fur child Tyson. A special education teacher in Prince George County, Virginia, she has been a reporter/columnist and freelanced for numerous publications. Passionate about dogs, Melissa is thrilled to share the tale of Waylon and Granny.

Eileen Gilmour ("Sleeping Dogs") was born in Liverpool, England, shortly after the Beatles. She now lives in an old country cottage with her husband and dogs. Her career in teaching has taken some surprising twists, and she recently launched her own reflexology school. She writes humorous material for women's magazines, anthologies, and literary competitions.

Betty Jo Goddard ("Under the Hemlock Tree") retired from teaching in 1983 and now lives on a ridgetop in Alaska with her three huskies. In her retirement years, she's taken up writing. This hobby gives her fun, a chance to share, and, when she tosses her lines in the publishing world's waters, enough bites to keep her dogs well fed.

T'Mara Goodsell ("Griswold the Talking Dog"), an ardent supporter of the Humane Society and a lover of mixed-breeds, writes, teaches, and lives with her two teenagers and Buddy, a Lab-terrier mix, outside of St. Louis, Missouri. She has contributed to previous *Cup of Comfort*® books as well as to other anthologies.

Catherine Grow ("Dog Asana") is a retired college teacher and writer happily co-existing with her husband and two large, mixed-breed dogs (Caleb, her co-yogi, and Cody, his non-yogic "brother") in a tiny, two-hundred-year-old house in rural northeastern Connecticut. Her work has appeared in a variety of small journals and college-level composition texts.

Betty Hard ("Show Time!") lives in Ontario, Canada, where, as an octogenarian, she enjoys gardening, crafting, and performing with The Entertainers music and dance troupe. After participating in a writing workshop at the local public library, she penned her first published piece, which appears in *A Cup of Comfort*® *for Adoptive Families*. She is now writing her memoirs as a legacy for her five grandchildren and three great-grandchildren.

Ann Hoffman ("My Perfect Nursemaid") is a retired lecturer of English literature and music. Her hobbies are singing, patchwork quilting, and writing. She has five children and ten grandchildren and lives with her husband in a small coastal town in South Africa.

Erika Hoffman ("For Dog's Sake!") has been published in several anthologies, including three *Cup of Comfort*® books, in several magazines, including *Australian Catholic Magazine, Today's Caregiver, 15-501 Magazine*, and *Come to the Fire*, and in newspapers. She makes her home in Chapel Hill, North Carolina, where she continues to take care of her son's dog.

Ramona John ("To Mugs, With Love") was judge of a juvenile court. Now retired, her published works include two books, magazine and newspaper articles, and stories in journals. She lives in Texas with her husband, Dick, and their two dogs, matronly German shepherd, Greta, and rescue dog, Jake, the mutt who makes them smile.

Christine Kettle ("An Autumn Romance"), a native of Glasgow, Scotland, has been married for more than thirty years and has lived in a small town in Ontario, Canada, for most of them. She's always had a love for reading but only recently discovered a love for writing too.

Joan King ("The Recruiting of Sergeant Berg") was raised on an Oklahoma farm that has been in her family for one hundred years. She recently had a short story chosen as a semifinalist for the Katherine Anne Porter Prize for Fiction and is currently working on a novel. She lives in Florida with her husband and beagle.

Kate Langenberg ("Fresh Out of Control") is an editor and writer living in Boston, Massachusetts, with her husband and their dog, Moses. She grew up in the Lehigh Valley in Pennsylvania and is a graduate of the University of Pittsburgh, where she studied English and writing.

Cathi LaMarche ("Blue Ribbon Winner") is the author of the novel *While the Daffodils Danced*. Her short story "Thief of Hearts" was published in *A Cup of Comfort*® *for Divorced Women*.

While pursuing her master's degree in teaching, she continues to work on her second novel. She resides in Missouri with her husband, two children, and two spoiled dogs.

Rolland Love ("Best Quail Dog in the Ozarks") grew up in the Ozark Mountains, where he spent summers helping his uncle run a fishing camp on the Jacks Forks River. He is the author of award-winning novels and short stories. He's also created monologues that he performs for schools, libraries, and business events.

Maryann McCullough ("The Convert") is a retired teacher from Phoenix, Arizona. A new writer of memoir and personal essays, she recently learned that her maiden name (Shanahan) comes from the Gaelic for storyteller and feels that, at sixty-six, she has found her true calling. Her work has been published in periodicals such as *Quiet Mountain Essays, Long Story Short, Monsoon Voices, and Underwired.*

Susan H. Miller ("The Dachshund That (Almost) Conquered the World") has loved to write since she was a small child. Although she refuses to limit herself to one genre, she admits her favorite stories come from her own experiences. She currently lives by a lake in Coldspring, Texas, venturing out to work occasionally as a nurse-case manager.

J.J. Morgan ("Gizmo's Way") lives with her husband, four children, and two dogs in the Chicago suburbs. A freelance writer, she is currently working on a novel. As for Gizmo, he continues to keep the family safe from four-legged predators.

Gary Presley ("Cooking for Dogs") resides in the Ozarks. His essays have appeared in Salon.com, *Notre Dame Magazine,* the *Ozark Mountaineer,* and other venues. He's also published numerous op-ed pieces on disability rights as well as a memoir, *Seven Wheelchairs: A Life Beyond Polio* (University of Iowa Press, 2008).

Darcy Purinton ("What's Good for Lily Is Good for Me") is a mom, freelance writer, and school counselor who lives in northern Vermont, where she feeds, chases, and adores Lily's puppies. She recently published her first book, *Tobacco Sheds of the Connecticut River Valley*, which she co-created with good friend and fellow dog lover, Dale Cahill.

Kelli L. Robinson ("Girl's Best Friend") lives in North Carolina and enjoys writing about life observations from a parent's perspective. She is a syndicated humor columnist and has written family-focused articles for local publications. Her husband, kids, and pets bring her happiness and supply new essay topics on a daily basis. Life is good.

Marcia Rudoff ("Eric's Champion") dreamed, as a child, of becoming a brain surgeon but wisely settled on teaching and writing as safer ways to get inside people's heads. Her stories, essays, and humor pieces have appeared in magazines, newspapers, and anthologies. She lives in Bainbridge Island, Washington, where she writes for the town newspaper and teaches memoir writing.

Mary Rudy ("I.Q. Test") writes from her home overlooking the San Francisco Bay. She has two children and two dogs and enjoys traveling to Mexico with her husband. Now that her son and daughter are in college, she has time to pursue her lifelong love of writing.

Kristin Seeman ("Bulldozer of Love") is a retired lawyer, living in Berkeley, California. She has raised seven great kids, five of whom are adopted, and has seven terrific grandchildren. She currently lives with her husband and two dogs, Mac and Cheeni, and enjoys travel, painting, and writing.

Rebecca Sims ("Serendipity on Four Legs") is a copywriter and freelance writer living near Cincinnati, Ohio. When not working, she can usually be found at the gym, a baseball game, or enjoying time at home with her husband, two children, and two dogs.

Marilee Stark ("Since I Fell for Chuck") is a writer and psychotherapist in the San Francisco Bay area. She writes a blog for Writing Mamas Salon and contributed a story to *A Cup of Comfort® for Single Mothers*. Marilee recently returned from a residency at One Writer's Place, where she worked on her memoir, *Mothering from the Inside Out*.

Linda Stork ("Penny's Protection") lives in the country outside of Eugene, Oregon, with her three dogs. She taught preschool through college for more than twenty-five years. Now she works part-time and spends lots of time reading, writing, and training her dogs in obedience, agility, therapy service work, tracking, and herding.

Susan Sundwall ("The Dog Who Knew My Name") is a freelance writer and children's playwright. She lives in Upstate New York with her husband and Libby. She is inspired daily by her kids, dogs, and grandkids, and is working hard on her second cozy mystery.

Ann E. Vitale ("No Job Training Required"), an award-winning member of Pennwriters, has been published in nonfiction, short fiction, and news columns. She lives in Pennsylvania and teaches writing at cultural centers and adult groups. None of her life experiences as a microbiologist, Ford dealer, or master gardener would have helped her the night her Newfoundlands came to her rescue.

Samantha Ducloux Waltz ("All in the Family") is an award-winning freelance writer who formerly wrote under the names Samellyn Wood and Samantha Ducloux. Her essays can be seen in numerous *Cup of Comfort*® books and other anthologies. She lives with her husband, Ray, her dog, Annie, and her cat, Naomi, in Portland, Oregon. Her horse, Vida, lives nearby.

Melinda L. Wentzel ("Wag the Dog") is a freelance writer and slice-of-life newspaper columnist whose primary aim is to unearth the humor contained within everyday life experiences. She and her husband reside in Williamsport, Pennsylvania, with their three daughters, two cats, and extraordinarily pampered dog.

Lois Wickstrom ("Buffy, the Pigeon Slayer"), of Philadelphia, Pennsylvania, is a computer-repair technician, a magician, and the creator of geezer-chick.com and lochness-monster.com. She also teaches science on ImagenieScienceAndMagic.com. Her book *Oliver, A Story About Adoption* won the Read America Award. Her latest book is *Amanda Mini-Mysteries*.

About the Editor

Colleen Sell is the anthologist of more than thirty volumes of the *Cup of Comfort*® book series. She has also authored, ghostwritten, or edited numerous other books; published scores of articles in periodicals; and served as editor-in-chief of two award-winning magazines. She and her husband, T.N. Trudeau, share an historic turn-of-the-century farmhouse, which they are perpetually renovating, on forty acres, which they are slowly turning into an organic blueberry, holly, and lavender farm, in the Pacific Northwest.